CATCH US THOSE LITTLE FOXES

CATCH US
THOSE LITTLE FOXES

by
A CARMELITE NUN

Author of

*Heartbreak Earth, Our Eternal Vocation, God and Rosanne,
World Without End, Each Hour Remains*

"Catch me the Fox, the little Fox there,
thieving among the vineyards; vineyards of
ours, all a-blossoming!"

Song of Songs, 3, 15

HENRY REGNERY COMPANY
CHICAGO

Nihil Obstat: HUBERTUS RICHARDS, S.T.L., L.S.S.
CENSOR DEPUTATUS

Imprimatur: E. MORROGH BERNARD
VIC. GEN.

Westmonasterii, die 2a Julii, 1954

First published in America 1955

HENRY REGNERY COMPANY
20 W. JACKSON BLVD.
CHICAGO 4, ILLINOIS

MADE AND PRINTED IN GREAT BRITAIN BY
NORTHUMBERLAND PRESS LIMITED
GATESHEAD ON TYNE

CONTENTS

12.5 a.m.

THE END OF A VIGIL

THE vigil is over and the day begins. The moonlight floods the choir as we turn towards the cloister, and the spring night is almost warm. Not every day begins for us with a vigil, or perhaps one should say that not every night ends with one, but there is a special loveliness about those which do. The meeting of night and morning: the end of one and the first promise of the other: both of them caught and held in the grace and warmth of the Blessed Sacrament which for an hour has been our Companion in the silent chapel beyond the grille.

Nuns are used to getting in and out of bed quickly, the bell for prayer and for the Divine Office sees to that for us, but sleep itself depends upon more than the simple act of going to bed. Aeroplanes are apt to dispute the mastery of the night with that other competitor, sleep. This night the aeroplanes seem unashamedly about to win. Up they flash at measured intervals into the sky. The stars themselves begin to move, or so it seems as, passing and repassing each other, they play hide and seek together. The dull red of the aeroplane lights shines against the greenish gold of the stars, while miles below, almost on a level with one's eyes, the pale emerald blobs of the spring trees show against the moon.

Lying here, under the whirr and thud of the engines, sleep recedes, but beneath the stars sleep does not seem to matter so much somehow; for this is a noise and a sense of stir which unites one to that world for which one prays. Actually there is more for God in it than in the old, quiet sleep of twenty

9

years ago, or even than in the deliberate vigil undertaken for some set purpose or intention. For this is the world itself—calling—imploring—as restless above as it is beneath. There is no mistaking the thud of its pulsing heart, while here, in quietness and peace, enclosed in a little world of darkness underneath the moon of God's creation and the clash of man's dealings with the skies in which it is set, rises the tiny link which unites earth to heaven, binds man to God, with a thin little spiral of prayer.

The steady beat and rhythm of the engines as the planes pass overhead remind one that all life is set to some rhythm or other, differing with each one personally, but supremely important to us as individuals. Some of us have a strong rhythm like the engines above, some a mere weak flutter of syncopated melody, some a series of spasmodic efforts followed by a dying pause. The whole affair is half psychological, half physical, I reflect serenely, with the serenity of being firmly settled where no particular effort is required for the moment, and where one's rhythm, in any case, is slowing down gently and pleasantly in the direction of sleep.

It is a good thing for us that nothing particular happens when our own personal rhythm falters, as would happen in the case of those apparently carefree pieces of mechanism careering overhead. "What *would* happen anyway?" I ask myself suddenly, as two of them roar past apparently chasing each other across the sky. I presume that they would come down on my head, but even that pleasant thought leaves me unmoved while poised between the beauty of a vigil and the dawn.

The important thing about our rhythm is, of course, not so much its importance to ourselves as to other people. Among any set of individuals, obliged for some reason or other to be much together, it is the strongest personality which is likely to set both the pace and the pitch for all the rest. The strongest, let us notice, and not necessarily the best. For rhythm may be of various kinds: the rhythm of habitual calm and order: the rushing, infectious sequences of enthusiasm and zeal : the jerkier stacatto of impulse and caprice : the slow, dull thud of routine or—which God forbid—the sobbing cadences of pain. All these are mainly psychological, but the only rhythm really worth having is the supernatural rhythm of unselfish, happy love.

Love is always supernatural in its essence whenever it is true love, and its rhythm is the best of all to be subject to, whether it be only the rhythm of human love at its highest, touched by the grace and the beauty of the love of God, or that deepest of all loves, the supernatural charity of Christ Himself on earth, and of His saints who live after Him.

The mere *tempo* of any rhythm must never, of course, be confused with the actual rhythm itself, for our *tempo* may vary to any extent, according to the necessities of the moment and the state of our health and spirits, without in the least affecting the essential beat of the unchanging metre. A solemn measure may occasionally quicken up, or a gay one be momentarily subdued, without altering the fundamental attuning of our lives to the measure which is characteristically ours, and which may so easily and unconsciously become that of others as well if we live much with other people.

The great thing to be avoided, of course, for all those living in community, is that disastrous thing called rocking the boat. We all know the type of person who stands up and waves her arms excitedly at every moment of crisis, and her companion in common sense who, in order to be better heard while she cries "Sit down!" rises and sways heavily as the rest of us cling to the gunwales.

The intervals between the planes overhead are becoming longer and longer; they have a way of going home to bed somewhere about one; and in the growing silence there comes into my mind the thought of an old Religious to whom I once had the privilege of being infirmarian. She ate but little, and had her meals alone up in the infirmary, where every day her dinner began with a bowl of very simple soup. One morning a small but special tin of *consommé* had been given us, and I had the bright idea of preparing it for her.

After a moment: "Is it good, Sister?" said I. She smiled. "It is different," she admitted. "You don't care for it!" I cried: "It is *different*," she repeated, "but that does not mean that it is either better or worse, little Sister. I just noticed the difference, that is all, but I should not have mentioned it if you had not." I said nothing because there was nothing to say.

"What does the taste of it matter? To me it is just the soup we have to-day—that is all." She laughed.

There was something about the infinite patience, the infinite serenity of her voice and eyes, which pierced even my youthful nonchalance as to the point of view of the old and the sick. I slipped from the room; seized a hot kettle and a bowl, put the usual little spoonful of Marmite at the bottom of it and poured on the water. It was just as she had it every day. I got back with it almost before she had time to notice that I had left the room, and whisked the other bowl from in front of her.

"Oh, but you shouldn't!" she exclaimed, really distressed, as she certainly had not been by the high flavouring of the first. "You don't understand: I really meant it; don't you see, little Sister, it is always perfect whatever God sends; we take no notice if it is good or bad if He sends it; it is just the soup that we have to-day—that is all."

I turned on my side the better to say good night to the moon: just such a beautiful Paschal moon as must once have shone on the Garden of Olives.

Whatever He sends us. . . . Well, He took whatever He was sent, that is certain. Cannot we do the same? Health or sickness for us poor mortals, success or failure, all that we need of this world's goods or too little for our human satisfaction. Snubs and oblivion or the precarious pleasure of apparent success. That is what the saints understood so well: they accepted it all from God, just as it came.

A last sleepy thought crawls through my mind. She had said no more than that, but, because she had said it so patiently and so pleasantly, I had found myself running down those stairs to mix her a brew better suited to her needs. Man is but made in the image of God and there is no kind impulse which comes to the human heart which has not come first straight from His. Is *that* it?—I mean, is that perhaps why all the lives of the saints seem to flow so harmoniously, in spite of human failures and miseries, often even of earthly scorn, towards their final end?   Everything working together for good, and all coming out right at the last—the eternal last, that is—just like an old-fashioned child's fairy-tale?

" Just the soup that we have to-day, dear Lord," they tell Him perhaps in the secret of their souls, and God turns and gets out His Marmite pot filled with just what suits them best. I wonder . . . and so, wondering, fall asleep.

4.45 a.m.

THE DAY'S FIRST PRAYER

THE *matraque* whirrs with that strange sound which wakes Carmelites to a new day, and for which I was pleasantly pre-pared on my arrival as a Postulant by the warning : it will sound like a ton of coal being delivered at your door. It does.

Let your first thought be of God, we are always told in Religion, for that will set the theme for the rest of the day. And indeed it is true. I remember a girl I knew in the world, who told me that although she worked in a busy office and had to give her whole attention to what she was doing, yet the sense of her early morning Mass never left her entirely. If she heard a bicycle bell as she went out to lunch, its tinkle was sufficient to bring back to her all the grace of the hushed church in spite of the roar of the traffic around; and the moment she waited for all day was the moment when, on her way home again, sometimes late, sometimes early, she could slip into the quiet chapel of some nuns with Perpetual Adoration, and kneel for a few minutes before the Blessed Sacrament.

Just an ordinary London business girl, but she knew something which many of us might be glad to know: how to begin her day aright and to hold it there until its close. Each day is only one day in a long sequence, when all is said and done, and so, one supposes, when she comes to die, the same will be true for all her life.

To begin the day aright is most emphatically to begin it with prayer, and to follow that up with the Mass. The prayer may only last for a brief moment or two, or it may last for an hour, according to our circumstances, but it is enough to offer to God the day's work, the day's trials, the day's successes, so that everything in it will belong to Him, as it should by right, and nothing be left out. It is the act of the will which matters, the offering of everything to God and for God: after that it is mainly a matter of following the grace of the moment.

The grace of the moment is a very wonderful thing. It comes with each duty, or pleasure, or fresh effort of any kind, and it is exactly proportionate to the purpose for which it is given. We shall often find, for instance, that, at the end of a long piece of work, we suddenly begin to go very much faster and with an ease which is quite new. We could not imagine ourselves beginning any set project at that pace, it would seem fantastic for the start, and still less could we maintain it through all the weary middle. This is quite simply the grace of the end, that unconscious crescendo which carries us to a successful conclusion and is a matter of both supernatural and psychological tension, of pleasure at the achievement of a satisfactory effort—a last spurt so to speak.

So it is for most things in life, and one would love to think that one might have the grace to die to a Crescendo Fortissimo, as befits one going to meet Eternal Love, and not to a Rallentando, as is sometimes the fate, one fears, of those who have habitually wasted their grace during life. It is worth thinking of, perhaps.

We get the grace for each fresh thing, fresh turn of events, trial, duty, pleasure, effort; but instead of acting upon it at once, how often we try, by our plans and our home-made rules, and unconscious self-will, to construct, as it were, a reservoir, with pipes all over the place, to hold it. It is never of any avail for, as a matter of fact, we can neither store our actual grace nor postpone it; it is given us now, for the thing we have to do to-day, at this very hour. All we can do, if we do not use it, is to lose it. It is not applicable to anything else, for that other thing, when it comes, will require its own special grace, which again will vary with a precise and delicate variability straight from God. We must quite simply *use* our grace: that is the only thing to do if we want to live continually at full pitch spiritually. To take the grace of the moment for the moment's work, and—as far as possible, even in the perfectly ordinary Christian life—let the work be primarily the work of God. We have to live, of course, and most of us have to work for our living; but God knows that a great deal better than we do, and He is not likely to make the achievement of the one clash with the achievement of the other.

There is, however, one dishonesty into which it is never permissible to fall under any circumstances: and that is to use God's grace for our own ends. That is a theft which is unworthy of us and which, in the long run, will surely never bring with it anything but pain.

The choir is filled with the light of an early spring morning. With all the windows open to the south one might almost as well be in the garden, and the birds cry good morning to the sun from the topmost branches of every tree. As I kneel in the first faint sunlight, the first act is to thank God for the grace of one's vocation, while I can be happily certain that every other sister in choir is doing the same. God loves gratitude, and there is no greater grace for which to be grateful to Him than the grace of vocation, whatever that vocation may be.

Whenever we follow our true vocation, whether we are aware of it or not, we are rendering glory to God. It may be conscious or unconscious, but it is always praise of the Almighty, because it is following His divine plan for us, doing the thing for which He created us, fitting into His scheme. In this sense, vocation always brings with it its own grace. How many thousands of people in the world, and all over the world, would be surprised to know that they were praising their Creator by the mere act of following the path He meant them to follow, using the gift He gave them, and doing whatever they happen to have chosen supremely well, just because the gift and the choice come from Him!

They would raise their eyebrows no doubt; they would smile a superior smile; they would shrug their shoulders; but that would not in any way alter the fact. It is a praise which we cannot deny to God so long as we use His gifts and follow His plan for us. We may call it by every other name; we may try to steal the glory by glorying, as we think, in our own successes as if we were the authors of them; but nothing can alter the fact that these are the successes of the Divine Creator, and that His creatures are only displaying the wonders of God by showing what richness He has put into human nature, and what variety into human capacity.

Here we have the reason why people who are genuinely following their vocation usually do whatever they are doing so well, or, if not perhaps quite so well as they sometimes think, at all events so happily. It is because they are using the grace of God which goes with the gift and the call to use it— the grace which accompanies any action of God and enables us to fulfil His purpose.

The birds sing louder to the rising sun as though endorsing my early morning picture of a bright and happy world, but one is obliged to follow on to the slightly sobering question : how many people do, in fact, find and follow their real vocation?

We Religious . . . how fortunate we are, for we have not only found it, but have, as far as human frailty permits, positively chained ourselves to it! That in itself is a great grace, and how many people out in the world, doing so precariously the thing which they love, would give their whole fortune to know that they would be able to go on doing it, better and better, crescendo upon crescendo, until they died! That can be true of every Religious. If we miss it, we miss it by our own fault, for there is nothing between us and it but the missing of our daily proffered grace. Health and age do not affect the issue because neither affects the soul but only the body. The value of a Religious who is constantly growing in the love of God, is a value which increases with every hour lived, and which cannot help but increase since its measure is the love of God.

It is true that almost the same may be said of those who find and follow their genuine vocation in the world, and if they love God, indeed, then exactly the same may be said. More often it is only true—with a difference. Who does not remember the names of those past-masters in art whom the world still flocked to see, to hear, to follow and to love, when they were old, because of the supreme point of ability and perfection which they had reached in their own subject, and which the passage of the years could never mar. But, even so, upon what a thread such earthly success hangs! An accident, an illness, a failure of some human organ and sense, and the earthly part of their career is at an end.

And, how small a number of them there are! Names which shine out in history are few and far between. Yet we were all created for some individual purpose, within the greater purpose of our eternal salvation and, generally speaking, the quickest and surest way of reaching that purpose should, one would think, logically be open to us. Then how do we come to miss it?

And the answer, one supposes, is that the easiest way either to miss or to lose it is not to be sufficiently aware of its importance. That, after all, is how we come to miss and to

B

lose most things. First, of its immense importance to us, because it is our unique opportunity of doing the thing which we were created to do in the supernatural order. Then its natural importance to us also, because we shall so obviously do whatever we were created and equipped to do a great deal better than anything else which we might choose, or which might merely be chosen for us by others less wise and less loving than God. And further, its immense importance to those with whom we live, because a misfit is never a really happy person, nor a very congenial companion in any surroundings.

It is difficult to trace precisely what that unawareness consists in. Sometimes it arises from fear or nervousness: we get the opportunity but it involves a break-away from present circumstances and our courage fails us. We delay, we drift, and gradually the opportunity evaporates until, we hardly know how, it is no longer open to us. Or we set about considering the drawbacks to some new proposition. We forget that everything in life has its drawbacks and, finding small flaws in what is offered us, decide against what we may later discover to have been a chance in a lifetime.

But, in point of fact, if only we are wise enough to be on the lookout for it, it is not easy to miss our vocation, for, when we are young, it knocks at our door with astonishing persistence. Who does not know that idea which comes back and back into the mind? The particular way of life, or profession, or occupation, from which we never seem able to get away, but which is always turning up and meeting us in the most unlikely places.

"Funny how I cannot get away from those people, but they are not my sort," or "It is not in my line," we say gaily and carelessly. Well, that may be, but if, on reaching middle life, we still find ourselves without any particular vocation of our own, and having instead to spend our time and our energy on other people's, we may perhaps reflect a little ruefully on some of those lost opportunities which we dismissed so lightly when the leaves showed a brighter green upon the trees than they do now, and the sun looked down upon us benevolently from a blue sky.

If such reflections should lead us to the melancholy conclusion that we *may* possibly have managed to miss what we were really fitted for and intended to do in life, then what, we may ask, should be our next step? The next step is, quite simply, to find it, even at this late stage.

It is no good pretending that there is no age-limit to some vocations, because there quite obviously is. One must admit that it would scarcely be reasonable to begin to train for anything highly technical in the late forties; but there are a dozen vocations, including that first and loveliest of all vocations, the vocation to the Religious Life, for which there is almost no age-bar but only a capacity-bar, as witness the encouraging parable of the twelfth-hour labourers in the vineyard.

All we have to do, at whatever age we wake up to the supreme happiness of a followed vocation, is to waste no more time in useless regrets, but set ourselves to cultivate that particular sort of spiritual and psychological awareness, (which begins, first of all, with awareness of God's wonderful Providence) which will lead us to observe, instead of disregarding, all the little incidents and opportunities which, missed, pass so easily away and are lost, but, taken, may well set us on the right path for ever.

And, through all this, how patient God is with us! He only asks our *attention*. If we will attend to Him, He will do all the rest. We shall find that things begin to drop into our lap without any asking. In spite of our repeated blind refusals, in spite of our obstinacy and selfwill, up to the very moment of death God continues to invite, to persuade, to beckon.

Now there is one perfectly obvious way in which we can, or ought to be able to, detect if we are travelling on the wrong—or just not on the right—path through life. If there is a recurring: "If I were you I should" in our conversations with other people, we may begin to wonder. This persistent desire on the part of them all to tell us what they would do if they were us, can only mean one thing: whatever the facts may be, we are managing to give the *impression* that we are not in the right place nor engaged in the right occupation.

Of course we may indignantly exclaim that it is only the mistake of a lot of intolerable busybodies. Very well, then, so much the better. In that case it is quite easy to rectify their mass-mistake by convincing ourselves that our circumstances are just what we should have chosen if we had all the world to choose from, and that we are doing the one thing on earth which suits us best. When we have convinced ourselves of that, we shall find that quite automatically all the busybodies will begin minding their own business again and no longer be interested in us and our occupations. It is a curious fact, but it has only to be tried to be proved.

On the other hand, let us admit that what they suggest may quite possibly be true. Perhaps we are *not* making the best of life; not using our gifts to the greatest advantage; we are either misfits or merely forlorn drifters, and everyone else can see it except ourselves. All we do is to grumble in general about life, without making any whole-hearted attempt to grapple with it.

For we have only to turn to God: to think of Him and of our neighbour instead of thinking exclusively along our own lines. We have only to wake up and become aware of existence as a real thing, and God as a real Person, and ourselves as His creation, and the next event in our lives will be that our vocation will come walking down the road to meet us, and bump into us so heavily that even we shall no longer be able to pretend that we do not know what it is.

If we believe at all that God created us, then we must believe that He created us with some particular end in view, and if a particular end in view, then some means of arriving at it. Obviously the means must concern our daily life. We cannot reach Heaven by one tremendous leap, however much one might dream of it as possible on a May morning with the Host in the Tabernacle for one's Companion. Yet, if we go through life listening to that dear Companion, with our attention centred upon Him (and no work or occupation of ours will ever suffer from that cause) He will find a dozen ways of letting us know where His will and His preference for us lie, and therefore where our own greatest efficiency and happiness lie also. We all know the happiness of doing what we *can* do, and doing it well: but the happiness of doing what *God* wants us to do—could there be any happiness on earth comparable to that? Added to which, since it is God's will and choice for us, and all our nature and temperament were made and fitted for it, then we shall find that it comes to fit us as a glove fits a hand with wear.

Apart from our own, we might all of us have a little more charity perhaps about each other's vocations. It is difficult to visualize that anyone may like doing what we should not like to do at all. Those people on the opposite side of the road, for instance, beyond our high wall which shuts them out, would not like to be a nun, particularly an enclosed one, and they don't think this life is any of the things which I think it is; but then, can I grasp the unimaginable bliss of adding up rows of figures, or tying up parcels behind a counter, or getting myself blown up in atomical research work, which really must give some people pleasure because they deliberately choose that vocation, or practising scales for hours on end which, for some other people, appears a perfectly reasonable thing to do and worth getting up for in the morning.

The sister who is going to ring the bell for the beginning of the Hours gets up to leave the choir, which means that there are only three minutes more in which to thank Our Lord for a quiet beginning to a new day. A happy frame of mind is in itself a great grace, because the reverse attitude is so easy to fall into. The reverse is that dreadful business commonly known as getting out of bed on the wrong side. The weather is too cold or too hot; the hour is too early or too late; with a sudden shock of horror one remembers that this is the day upon which the tunics have to be washed, and one forgets all the things that the Little Flower said about trials; the laundry chimney will smoke as a matter of course, and the water will never get properly hot; someone else will have to supply for the work of those sisters who are washing; if one is not among the suppliers, then one will be a whole-day washer, and in this particular frame of mind, whichever falls to one's lot will inevitably be the harder. So it goes on all day. The hour of prayer spoilt, the Divine Office but peevishly recited; the pitch and the note of our whole day set, and set in a minor key.

And that, I suspect, is another reason why some people's vocations have never been found, and others, though found, have never been consistently followed. You can kill a vocation by constantly grumbling at it, just as you can kill love or happiness of any kind by constant grumbling. If we just did that which we were created to do, that which God invites us to do, that which, if we did it, in spite of the rough and the smooth, and the ups and downs of life, would make us so supremely happy in ourselves and such pleasant companions for all those whom we met, half our problems would melt into thin air. For, as we said before, there is nothing like doing what we can do well for making us happy—and who could know better than God, when He breathed the soul into us, what that is, however much we may be tempted to think that it is something else.

We lose our ideals, we become disillusioned, and it is all so unnecessary. Every Christian is agreed that this earth and this life are only the way to Heaven for us, and how can one possibly be disillusioned on the way to Heaven, or lose one's ideal when that ideal is the very Heaven to which we are all on the way? If we are really disillusioned then it looks rather as if our reasoning had gone wrong somewhere. Either we have missed the path and are not on the way to Heaven at all, or we have got so tangled up in our following of it that we cannot, as the old proverb warns us may happen, see the wood for the trees.

If we were travelling to Lourdes or to Fatima, or to Rome

for a Holy Year, we should take all the misfortunes of the journey in our stride and with the gay mortification of proper pilgrims. Then what on earth and in the name of common sense is the matter with us when we wear long faces on our journey to God? Not just to His shrine, or to His Basilica, but to Him Himself. . . .

The bell for the Hours begins to ring. *"Aperi Domine"*. . .

6 a.m.

THE HOURS

THE rustle in the stalls subsides as we settle down to the recitation of the four Hours, Prime, Tierce, Sext and None. The expression, Divine Office, signifies a duty accomplished for God, and it is good to get that fact firmly established in one's head before beginning it. It is for this reason that many priests do not approve of the usage in France of the term "Saint-Office" as identical with "Office-Divin". There is more to it than the first expression would imply.

The practice of reciting prayers at certain fixed hours of the day or night goes back as far as the ancient days of the Jews, and in the Psalms we meet with many such phrases as "I will meditate on Thee in the morning": "I rose at midnight to give praise to Thee"; "Evening and morning and at noon I will speak and declare . . ." or again, "Seven times a day I have given praise to Thee".

The Apostles kept the Jewish custom of praying at midnight, Tierce, Sext and None. Actually, although our present-day Divine Office is infinitely more elaborate than it was in the beginning, it is nevertheless derived, by a process of normal and gradual change, from the primitive elements of the early Christian days. It is held by some authorities that the Mass of the Catechumens, which formed a prelude or vigil to the real Mass, is the original kernel of the whole Divine Office, and that it has slowly evolved from that into our present-day liturgy.

The beginning of the office of Prime is altogether less respectable, I am afraid, although actually it is the only Hour the precise origin and date of which are known. While turning to the right page in our Breviary I could not but ponder upon the regrettable fact that the fame of our ill deeds spreads much more rapidly than the fame of our good, for no one seems to know which were the particular saints who instituted the other Hours, but nearly everyone has heard of the deplorable sinners who were the cause of the institution of Prime. It dates from somewhere about the year 380, and the place of its origin has been identified as one or other of two monasteries situated not far from the Village of the Shepherds, outside Bethlehem.

Prime is undoubtedly the prayer of the beginning of the day: the prayer which consecrates all our work to God and orientates it towards its true end and purpose. But it began precisely because certain monks in one or other of those two monasteries saw fit to do no early morning work at all, but instead to sleep the sleep of the unjust. The Night Office in the monasteries of Palestine ended at sunrise, so that Lauds coincided with the dawn, after which the monks might retire to rest for a while. But this is where the sad part of the story begins for, there being no further Office to call them together before Tierce, which was said at nine o'clock, some of the monks continued to sleep until that Hour instead of rising as they should to engage in manual work or spiritual reading.

Undaunted by such a state of affairs, their wise and tactful Abbot, instead of falling upon the erring Brothers, merely recalled them all again to the choir at six o'clock for the Office of Prime, which he made up especially for them, and which at first consisted only of a few psalms (just enough, in fact, to get them out of bed and no more), after which they had no option but to continue to work until the recitation of Tierce at nine o'clock. After all, they could not very well go back to bed *again*.

As we cheerfully begin "*Jam lucis orto sidere*" it is pleasant to reflect that at this stage we are liturgically completely correct even from the strictest Benedictine point of view. We are saying Prime at six o'clock, and that is the time at which Prime ought to be said. After that, as to the times at which we say everything else, from the Benedictine point of view we are thoroughly feminine and past praying for.

When I was a Novice we had an old French sister to whom, in our lighter moments and on special occasions of unbending such as Christmas Day, we used to sing "Three Blind Mice". Compared to the French equivalent of "*Mon frère Jacques*" it sounded, of course, uncouth in the extreme and, covering her ears with her hands, she insisted that it was "enough to make the hair dress on the head". Well, our method of reciting the Divine Office makes the hair of a Cistercian dress on his head. Some of us have Cistercian brothers, so we know.

The fact is, the great St. Teresa of Avila was a saint, and a reformer, and an ardent daughter of the Church, combined with being a wonderful contemplative; but she was not of a fussy disposition. No doubt she had her own reasons for arranging the hours of the Divine Office as she did, but they were certainly not Benedictine reasons, and one may perhaps secretly sympathize a little with the correct liturgists.

One of the reasons which she gave quite openly for fixing the hour of Matins at nine o'clock, and deciding that her daughters should not rise for the Midnight Office, as do the Fathers, but instead have an exceedingly long day on end—to be precise nearly eighteen hours in winter and nineteen in summer without rest; that is to say a bare six or seven hours of sleep, according to the season of the year—was that no other Order of Religious said the Divine Office at that particular time of night. They did not: but that never seemed to strike her as a reason why she should not: quite the contrary. It was, she felt, a time at which those in the world required much extra prayer to keep them safe from the follies and the sins of the night. That is a thought which may still console and strengthen many a modern Carmelite, struggling perhaps with a certain weariness after a long day's work. " Your fatigue prays better than you ever could," our old Mistress of Novices used to assure us smilingly.

With the beginning of Sext I make my Intention afresh : all the Intentions of the Holy Father, and especially his Intention for those Catholics struggling, perhaps under difficulties, to keep their faith in the faithless world of to-day. For surely belief—in anything—is the difficulty of the present generation. Believing that the earth is still the earth which God created, and set in order, and loves, in spite of the disorder and hate into which it has fallen. Believing in other people when we know that we cannot. Believing them capable of a virtue which we know they do not possess, and a straightness which we know is not in their character. We are right : they have not got those qualities, and they are not even striving for them : but if we refuse to believe them capable of changing, if we refuse to go on praying hopefully for them, and encouraging them, then we refuse to believe in the grace and the power of God.

We must believe in the improbable, just as Our Lord had once to believe in it on earth : to believe in those who betrayed Him, as they still betray us and make us suffer. That is the meaning of Christianity. It is God in whom we believe —seeing Him in them. It is God in whom we have to trust; and if we turn our backs on them then we are turning our backs on Redemption.

Broken faith everywhere—and a Catholic goes on believing in God and his fellow-men. Broken hearts all round—and a Catholic goes on believing in love. Broken trust, and honesty of purpose, and truth, lying the whole length of the road— and a Catholic picks up the pieces, and puts them together, and goes on believing in them. The faith and the love and the truth of God are enough for us : for the rest, we are content with what fragments we can find among the world's débris.

And in those whom we meet on the journey of life, let us never disregard the "beggar-look" in eyes. The beggar-look? It is just that: no other words describe it—faint hope and desperate longing; wistful searching and the fear of a rebuff —and always, I think, it means that, at some point, life has played them false. Never let those people go without the word of sympathy, the hand held out, for there is real need behind that look. It is not suspicious, not unfriendly: but it is the look of one who, at some time, has asked and been refused. It always means pain in the soul—though the pain, by now, may be very old.

It is a look and a touch that would have made Jesus turn; that would have drawn from Him one of His most wonderful and utterly gratuitous miracles: it is the cry of weakness appealing to strength; of anguish calling upon peace; of want begging from abundance. Christ always gave of His strength, His peace, and His abundance, and we are His poor followers, after all.

"*Divinum auxilium maneat semper nobiscum*" says the Hebdomadary as we close our Breviaries at the end of None.

7.15 a.m.

WORK BEGINS

THE first work of the day varies, in my particular case, very much with the time of the year, the light, and the weather. At this time of year it is the garden when the morning is fine, and that gives me an opportunity to pull up all Sister Rose's best plants by mistake for weeds, without her being able to say a word in protest as she surely would later on in the day. It is true that with the end of the Martyrology at Prime the official silence of the night is over, but the moderated silence of the day begins, and, especially before Mass, it is only a matter of the greatest necessity which compels us to speak to one another.

As I go towards the principal summer-bed, which is the hope of her heart for June and July, I resolve to set her mind at ease for one morning at least. For with whatever agony she might watch me performing the crime, so holy is Sister Rose that I am quite sure she would see every budding—now, that is just the trouble, because for the life of me I cannot remember if it is lilies, carnations, wallflowers, or what, which do bud in June! I decide in favour of what, but as I do not know what what looks like, how am I to avoid pulling it up? Meanwhile, my compassionate soul tells me that, having seen the direction my steps are taking, Sister Rose is offering up mingled prayers and groans at the rate of several hundreds a minute. I shrewdly suspect that her holy eye is glued upon me from somewhere in the direction of the house, so, turning towards it, I wave the rake and the trowel reassuringly in my two hands, bring them together in a gesture of profound supplication, raise my eyes to heaven intimating that I will join my prayers to hers, and bow profoundly in token of humble respect for her wishes. Whether Sister Rose has understood all that is another matter, but at least she must be aware of the purity of my intentions.

At this stage it is almost superfluous to ask whether I enjoy gardening, for surely the answer must already be abundantly clear, but what would be quite a reasonable question to ask, is what any Religious should do with her likes and dislikes, her aptitudes and disabilities, either in the matter of work or anything else? It is perfectly simple : in common with every other sensible person, she should take no notice of them whatsoever. As for our disabilities, we shall soon get to know of those without any further effort on our part.

We do our work in life, wherever we are, because the work

needs doing, and because we have either chosen, or been chosen, to do it. And for just that reason, that it is work which needs doing and which, if we do not do it, will either fall to the ground, or fall to the share of someone more charitable than ourselves who will have to make good for us, we do it to the very best of our ability, with all our attention, and with all the skill which we have. No one can do more than that: and no one should do less.

One is not, of course, alluding to work done solely for money, and which can therefore be nobody's actual vocation, for vocational work is always done mainly for love, and if money is involved in the transaction as well, so much the better, particularly for other people to whom we shall then be no burden; but let us be clear as to the fact that the money makes no difference to the love either one way or the other. It is fairly obvious that the less anyone thinks of the money, and the more they think of the work, and of their employer, and of those who are going to benefit by the work, the better their work will be.

Now our employer is God, and our beneficiaries are all the souls in the world who need prayers, so it is to be hoped that we can set out to our tasks, at whatever time and in whatever weather, with a good heart and a cheerful determination to do our best whether we like it or not.

The first hour of work sets the pace and the mood for the rest of the day, for it will take hours to pray ourselves and shake ourselves out of a disgruntled frame of mind, whereas the swing of a good beginning will still be with us when a tired but welcome evening comes at last. There are one or two obvious pitfalls which prevent us from putting our best into whatever we are doing : one is the habit of looking too much to others for our incentive, and another is that great fault of to-day—" to-morrow ". Everyone lives for to-morrow —to-morrow which is just to-day over again.

If only in all such matters we could see ourselves as others see us, how easy it would be to set ourselves right! We can always set everyone else right, so why not ourselves? Now the curious thing about it is that, when we are dead, we shall undoubtedly see ourselves (most of us for the first time and with considerable shock) as others see us, *and we shall agree with them*. It is quite unthinkable that they should all be wrong and we alone be right, particularly when we consider that they are actually looking at us, and hearing us, and having to live with us, whereas we are so situated as to make it practically impossible for us to get any real idea of the impact which we make upon others. If only we could get the bump of our own impact upon ourselves for one day, we should probably be nicer, and wiser, and humbler people for the rest of our lives.

But, since God has arranged things so that personal experience is impossible, at least we can get the impression of that impact at second-hand; and—if we ask for it—at a by no means too remote second-hand; for there are far more people in the world who desire to impart the truth to others—particularly about themselves—than there are others wishing to receive it.

When we are all dead, Sister Mary So and So will see herself from my point of view, and I shall see myself (and my teeth chatter in advance) from Sister Rose's. So why not begin to agree with their verdict now, while there is still time to change? It will be tragic only to see the truth of it when it is too late to do anything to alter ourselves.

Under the influence of the thought I find myself looking feverishly through the growing pile of weeds lest some of the wheat should have got among the tares, and when I find that it undoubtedly has, I hastily replant it while my eyes bulge with horror as I surreptitiously press the earth down firmly again all round. But even as I pat the soil into place, I begin to wonder if, after all, it *is* a wheat, and fear that instead Sister Rose may find next June a cultivated and magnificent dandelion growing among her choicest specimens. It will not be difficult to visualize myself from her point of view if she does. Still, as the parable tells us, better one tare among the wheat than half a dozen good wheats among the tares, so whatever plant it happens to be now, may some miracle turn it into a beautiful carnation or lily or pansy before next summer comes. Such things have always happened in the lives of the saints and, as I reflect with the deepest satisfaction, Sister Rose is most probably a saint.

Another thing which sometimes prevents us from giving of our best to God and our fellow men is a certain sensitiveness, but sensitiveness is a two-edged quality which should never be condemned wholesale as it so often is. For the dictionary-meaning of the word is "the state of being delicately adjusted" or "the state of being readily affected by the action of appropriate agents", and that is a good and not a bad quality. Those who have a great awareness of God and of beauty and the hidden and delicious secrets of life, and the loveliness of both heaven and earth, have also the same awareness for things unpleasant—a consciousness which occasionally acts upon them as an almost overpowering shyness and deterrent.

They have to be on their guard against it, but on the whole it is far better to suffer temperamentally in that way than to be of the large company of the insensitive, who are aware of neither, and who are quite content to go through life joyously treading upon the toes of others, while gaily begging pardon without any apparent perception of the pain they have caused. Or—have they really no perception? One wonders. Is there not a shade of contempt for all sensitiveness mixed in with their apologetic bows and smiles, a contempt which entirely precludes sympathy with sensitiveness of any sort, and would seem often to include a certain satisfaction in being able to make the owners of it wince?

However, since to be sensitive always means in one way to be temperamental also, sensitive people have to keep a watch upon themselves. If they do not, they will suddenly find the temperament breaking through all the defences, and wearing itself on the outside—a thing which a temperament should never, never be allowed to do.

For the fact is (though plenty of rather rueful sufferers may be inclined to disagree) that temperament is a very pleasant and useful article to have *strictly for one's own use*. It makes life at least twice as real, as wonderful, and as humorous, as it is for those entirely devoid of it. But that is only the case if it remains where it takes birth, which is inside its owner. The moment it gets loose and begins to worry one's neighbour—and it always does worry one's neighbour—it is no longer an asset but an intolerable burden.

Now when an attack of temperament is coming on, there is always some sort of danger-signal, which varies with individuals but which soon comes to be easily recognizable. Recognized by the temperament-owner, that is, for, if they are wise, no one else will even guess of its existence. It is a danger-signal for their own warning: no one else's. With some it may take the form of a sensation of irritation, with others of fear, or even an attack of weeping or some physical *malaise* such as sickness or violent headache. That is the danger-signal, but it is not the cause as is so often presumed: the cause lies far beneath.

For one Sister, I know, it was ceremonies. The first flower for decorations was enough for her. She got to recognize the fact and, when she saw the distant preparations beginning, wisely made her own preparations too. With others it might just as easily be physical fatigue, or some special kind of work, or the proximity of a particular person, or a dozen things which crop up in the course of a day. But always there will be some prelude of physical reaction which soon comes to be familiar to those anxious to avoid all temperamental storms.

For instance, the Sister whose weak spot was ceremonies of any kind confided to me that she never tried to do anything positive to combat it, as she found that it inevitably made it worse. All she did—and did it very well as far as onlookers were concerned—was to live through the bad patch as tranquilly as she could, promising herself that, with patience, it must after all come to an end sooner or later. She did not attempt to persuade herself that she liked the occasion, nor reason with herself, nor over-emphasize the matter in any way—not even by enduring it with set teeth. She just lived through it as quietly as she could, as she would have lived through a bad attack of toothache or an air-raid or a thunderstorm.

That was certainly an unselfish approach to the temperamental difficulty and, when it comes to the point, unselfishness would probably be a solution to all problems of this sort. But unfortunately unselfishness does not grow upon every bush. There is no question of acquiring it by merely making up one's mind that it is a desirable virtue. One has to be *unselfish* in order to be unselfish, and that is just what most of us cannot manage to be. Concentration upon ourselves and our own virtues is obviously the last way of reaching it, since the whole point is that unselfish people hardly think about themselves at all except in relation to others. Perhaps from one point of view one could describe unselfishness as such an awareness of another person's position, predicament, feelings, difficulties, and mental approach, as to be able to see as another sees and feel as another feels, or at all events to realize how they see and feel, even if one has never felt like that oneself. Thus it can happen, and it is always kind to suppose that it has happened, that a person who appears selfish may be only a person with absolutely no imagination.

Real unselfishness should ultimately lead to one of the most precious virtues of all—that is, to detachment; and, contrariwise, the best test of the genuineness of detachment is whether it leaves us selfish or not. For the selfish indifference of the egoist is as far from the reality of genuine detachment as black from white. If, however, detachment goes hand in hand with unselfishness and charity, then it may be the beginning of the real and rare detachment which belongs to the spiritual life : a detachment which means that, whereas before things were done from natural motives and for human considerations, at least in part, they are now done by the grace of God and solely for supernatural reasons. There will be, for instance, no over-emphasis on results, no desire for gratitude,

C

no welcoming of praise, and equally no rejection of failure or blame.

In the case of a Religious, or of any soul aspiring to perfection, it is a point to be noted, because the indifference of the egoist, which develops quite easily in the early stages of religious, or any other type of spiritual life, is something which should be checked at once. The other—that is, real detachment—arrived at by means of the conformity of the the will with the will of God, accompanied by a marked degree of supernatural charity, must be left to grow slowly and as God Himself chooses. He will send the appropriate means and circumstances calculated to foster its growth.

The last stage of it is surely that stage sometimes reached by the saints. The stage where joy, unshared by them and even inconceivable to them in the darkness of their soul, is yet a strange, impersonal joy for the sake of others. A stage where they have no joy, can imagine no joy, and desire no joy, yet are infinitely concerned with the joy of other people. They can share, as it were, in the happiness of others, in one sense from afar and in another sense from very near, without one iota of personal participation in it. It is altruism in its highest form and surely one of the sweetest characteristics of the saints. For it knows no envy, no jealousy, no repining, no dissatisfaction of any kind, but only a great happiness that someone else should have joy, even were they never to have one second of joy again themselves.

8 a.m.

THE DIVINE SECRET

W E come slowly in procession into the dim choir for the
supreme half-hour of our day : the half-hour which gives
point and value to all the rest of it and makes it worth while.
This is the half-hour for which the beautiful Divine Office
last night (Vigils) was a preparation, and for which the rest
of our day will be a thanksgiving.

There are, if one pauses to reflect, so many views which
can be taken of the Mass; so many different graces which it
brings us as individuals according to our need; but most of
these are subject-matter for the theologian. For us, the Mass
is the complete and perfect central point of our life : not
alone in the religious sense as it is for every good Catholic
who goes to Mass daily, but in the complete sense of the word,
such as it would be if those Catholics were to include in the
joy of their Mass all the other pleasures which the hours
might hold in store for them : the meetings with friends; the
good book which they were waiting to finish; to-night's seat
at the Opera. Every joy, every hope, and every consolation,
compressed and held for us in that one shining half-hour.

On Sundays and the big Feasts of the Church, we draw our
thicker curtain between us and the outside chapel, have the
window-shutters of our Choir open, and chant the Mass from
our missals. On those days we cannot see the altar, but only
the roof of the chapel over the top of the thicker curtain.
(We come, of course, as usual to receive Holy Communion at
the small grille.) But on other days our window-shutters are
closed, we draw back all but the thinner curtain between us

35

and the Sanctuary, and we get a complete side-view of the altar and of the priest, although none at all of the congregation, not even enough to know if there is any. A dim figure moving to and fro represents to us the server, if there is one, and this we have to know since, if there should be none, a Sister would answer the Mass, kneeling in the shadows at the corner of the choir grille.

When first entering Carmel a postulant may feel a little strange in such surroundings, for our Mass is a dark Mass— its innermost secret held, intangibly but distinctly and individually, in the heart of each Carmelite. But after a few weeks the dark Mass comes to be the beloved Mass. I often wonder if the priest who officiates realizes how much he does for us : so circumscribed that we can get no other Mass but his; so dependent upon him that, were he to fail us, for that day our Lord would remain remote and unattainable out in the Tabernacle, and each of us here lonely.

When we have Exposition of the Blessed Sacrament in the chapel, we watch all day in turns before the open grille, but the loveliest Expositions for us are our Expositions in the private convent-oratory which lies at the back of the high altar and where, through an opening in the chapel wall, the Monstrance is placed upon a revolving circular platform and turned round to us inside. There our Lord remains with us all day, behind little golden bars on a level with the oratory altar, so that we can draw round Him with a nearness unknown to the Faithful in the world, and with no more than the tiny metal grille between us.

I often think of the peace of the intimate circle at Bethany, with our Lord, and Martha and Mary, and Lazarus and St. John, and one or two others of His disciples, and of the dusk falling as they talked together, and the birds calling good night as the long shadows grew. Then I wonder, as so many enclosed nuns must have wondered before me, why God is so good to us who deserve it so little, and why people in the world cannot see—see and understand the limitation of their idea of wasted lives and starved minds and souls. Who could be starved, who could be wasted, with the Lord of all Creation within a few feet of them, only waiting, as He waited at Bethany, so gentle and so condescending, to be asked and to give?   To give Redemption to all the world as He gave Redemption to the world then.

And this, perhaps, is how our everyday Mass seems to us too.   For us it does not mean so much the details of the liturgy, which we should not be able to follow in any case in our shadowy light, as a meeting of lovers: the love in the soul of the creature and the love in the soul of Christ for us.

The priest comes out of the Sacristy into the soft, blurred sunlight of the chapel.   There is a server this morning and together they move to the altar-steps.   Carmelites kneel quite simply on the floor through Mass—no slippery mats, no wooden kneelers to betray one suddenly with an unexpected tilt, no prie-dieu to creak and mutter at every movement—just the sunshine and the candlelight, shaded for us into palest gold by the semi-transparent curtain, cut into long vertical lines by the wooden bars of the grille.   That, and the Lord of all Creation waiting to give Himself to us.

11 a.m.

THE GARDEN IN MAY

THE May sun is hot as we come into the garden from the cool passages of the convent.   The early morning work is done; the dinner, early also as it would be in Spain, is finished; in little groups we find our way down to the circular stone seat where we usually sit for recreation, and where the as yet uncut grass is patterned, for all the world as though we were in the middle of some country field, with daisies and buttercups and little tufts of clover. Tall trees add to the illusion of the countryside and from this sunk lawn the sound of the distant traffic is no more than a pleasant murmur. A small swarm of wild bees which makes its home with us permanently, although we have never been able to find out exactly where it hides, has discovered the clover and the occasional cowslips, and in every cup there is a dusty little brown coat and a pair of busy legs or arms or whatever it is they use so eagerly.

In the old days of our Spanish Mothers, one of the Sisters would periodically sound a small clapper during recreation "to recall her companions to the thought of God", lest in their unaccustomed conversation they should allow themselves to get too far away from it. We have no formal rules for recreation, so far as I know (although many little customs of charity), beyond that one golden rule that we never altogether lose the remembrance of God; it is sufficient. But on the human side, I reflect, as the Sisters continue to arrive with their work-baskets, there is another golden rule also.

Never for a moment, or by a single sentence, should one say anything calculated, even in the remotest, most unintentional degree, to depress or to sadden others. Let us leave all the gilt on other people's gingerbread even if we have been so foolish as to lick it off our own. After all, we would not do anything to damage other people's physical health, and it is a far more serious thing to damage their spiritual or mental happiness. It is just as real an injury to cloud a person's spiritual outlook upon life, as it would be deliberately to cloud their physical sight. No one would dream of doing anything—if such were possible—to take the colour out of a landscape for someone else on a summer day, yet there are plenty of people who, without a qualm, will try to create a grey world of thought for others to live in.

One more thing, I say to myself, as a late Sister arrives and one notices the little stir with which her coming is greeted—slight certainly but unmistakable : for those who are possessed of that rare and elusive quality called personality, let them beware of how they use their gift whatever their sphere of life, but perhaps rather specially in a religious community.

It may be said that they are themselves unaware of it, and so they may be, in so far as they themselves do not, of course, feel the effects. Still, they cannot surely, if only by reason of other people's reaction to them, be *entirely* unaware of the gift. It is like a person who has a real voice : the moment they appear, the moment they join in any singing, wherever and whatever it may be, the singing turns into a concert. They can scarcely believe, one would imagine, however great their modesty, that it still remains the subdued and slightly dismal wailing which it was before their advent!

The plain fact is that some people arrive anywhere bringing the party with them, and when they go away the party goes away too so far as those left behind are concerned. I suppose if you perennially take your party about with you, you do not view your own absence in quite the same light as others; still, it is not a bad thing for such people to be at least faintly aware of the situation. They need not be self-conscious—indeed if they were, paradoxically no one else would probably be conscious of them at all—but at least they might be sufficiently aware of the gift as not to bring other people's concerts to a close too abruptly or without good reason, and not necessarily to take the party home suddenly with them every time they themselves feel that it has come to a desired end.

This party is coming to an end in any case because the time allowed for it is over and, with the ringing of the Angelus at twelve, we come to one of the most delightful hours in Carmelite life—the hour of summer midday silence. One has lived through a good many of them, yet their charm never decreases. Looking back, all the silences seem to me to have been golden : that is pure imagination, of course—it must have rained sometimes—but that is the effect left on my mind. It is an hour packed full of all the lovely things which one can do in it—work—read—pray—think—love God :

indeed, all the time love God whatever else one does as well. There are two hours in Carmel as near to Heaven as one can get on earth. The hour of midday Silence and the midnight hour of night.

1 p.m.

NOVITIATE DAYS

HELPING the Novices to "mark" their Divine Office is a duty which happily—or unhappily—falls to my share on most days of the week. I say unhappily because although marking one's own office is one thing, subsequently performing in choir what one has marked is quite another. One has to tell the Novices to listen respectfully to all that is said, and to receive it as from an oracle, but to turn a blind and charitable eye to what is ultimately done when we all arrive together in choir.

As Hebdomadary anyone may be safe enough, because Hebdomadaries have little to do with anything but prayers and benedictions; but when it comes to a Cantor and anti-phons, first one never knows whose turn it is to announce them; nor, next, who it is to announce them to; nor which it is to be announced. It is even related, although I do not myself believe it, that on one occasion a bewildered Cantor advanced up the choir and halted opposite a Sister with a desperate: "I haven't the least idea, Sister, please choose for yourself . . ." which the other most obligingly did.

Be that as it may (and I trust it was not) the fact remains that at the moment it is my pleasing duty to try and get the Divine Office, and a great love for it, into the heads of the Novitiate, and that incidentally at the same time a good deal comes out of their heads which I find almost as interesting as the Divine Office itself; for what comes out is what they think, just as they think it.

Our Holy Mother St. Teresa said that what one is in the Novitiate, one will always remain. When one remembers what one was in the Novitiate it is a little depressing to know that one is always going to be like that : but the Novices themselves, I notice, when they have this sage remark read out to them, seem quite pleased with the idea, and even a little inclined to congratulate the rest of us upon it. Such a support for us to look forward to, I think they feel. All that comes out of their heads is nice, but there is always that fundamental trouble of Newman's real and notional assents. We must *believe* our own principles, not just think them, if they are to be of any use to us, for holiness rests upon belief and never upon thought alone.

Between the Professed Sisters and this post-war generation of Novices there are quite noticeable differences in outlook, but the same old principles which have served generations of Novices still hold good. The great difference between at least the *manner* of their coming into Religion and ours is that we left a lovely world, and they apparently do not. It is an interesting world perhaps, and a world in which it is easy enough to be ambitious with hope that the ambitions may be realized, but it is not that world of culture and beauty and leisure which we knew.

The result—a little astonishingly—is that at the outset they have fewer difficulties to encounter than we had. Naturally speaking, they find the life quite attractive : it has a peace, a calm, and a certain orderliness which they find soothing. That is the English reaction, perhaps, more than the Continental, since books by Continental writers would seem to suggest that postulants find the life exteriorly restrictive, and do not breathe the sigh of relief which ours do at the absence of flurry. Of course one must remember that their war was a shorter affair than ours, and also that there may not be the absence of flurry.

Another difference is that we came into Religion very much on our own initiative, whereas they almost give the effect of having to be fetched. We should have been repelled, I think, by any attempt to suggest our vocation to us, whereas, in some cases at least, they seem to regard it as almost a necessary sign that they have one. It is always dangerous to try and generalize in such matters, and these are only the mildest of suggestions which I make to myself as to present-day trends, but in any case there is a very simple reason why they might be the truth.

The modern girl has been trained to have a very just appreciation of her own usefulness, and the necessity of having a use. In our day it was not considered a social crime to be purely ornamental: now it is. Consequently the modern postulants are anxious to be assured that they are wanted before they ask to come. They have grown so accustomed to being directed to where there are shortages— if not in actual fact at least by public opinion—and headed off from where there are redundancies, that they want to be certain, so to speak, that the Church is really short of nuns before they make up their minds to see if there is anything they can do about it.

Well, God and the Church are always short of the right kind of nun, they can make their minds easy as to that, but, as one assures them daily, they must *be* the right kind. Spiritually speaking one can say that they must love God very greatly—genuinely more than anything else on earth—and be prepared to sacrifice everything for His sake : but that still leaves all the details to be filled in. Life in the Novitiate will fill them in with time, and no doubt the details differ a little with every separate Order; still, there are one or two broad principles which surely apply to all Religious.

Any form of ambition will ruin everything from the outset —even spiritual ambition. We come into Religion to give and not to get : to lose and not to gain. Supernaturally we get and gain everything in God, but actually we give and lose everything from the natural point of view. As the treasure and the wealth increase, so do the gift and the loss increase also. The two are in direct ratio one to the other. Where there is any attempt to seize and enjoy spiritually, without the corresponding willingness to lose and to give, there are potential causes of disaster.

Another snare is the love of our own will, however deeply hidden—indeed the more deeply concealed the more dangerous. We should spare ourselves a good deal of trouble in Religion if we could only accept, once and for all, the simple and obvious fact that if one person says we are wrong, we probably are; if two people say we are wrong, then we almost certainly are; and if three people say we are wrong, then there is no further question about it, we *are* wrong. Why should we not be?

Of the two general tendencies, from one of which nearly all of us suffer for it is rare to find a perfectly balanced temperament, that is half-heartedness and over-zeal, the former is surely the more dangerous. Over-zeal is of course apt to show itself in later years in the form of irritability and hastiness of temper, but one must not forget that there is, even so, temper and temper. One kind does very little harm. The temper that is almost purely physical and nervous does not rest in the *mind* : it never turns bitter, it never wishes to injure; it has no roots in the soul and is a completely exterior affliction. But the moment a temper smoulders—that is something quite different. That is temper which begins, not in involuntary nervous reactions, but in a deep-seated discontent of the soul.

Such temper, in a Religious at all events, is in its essence temper with God. It is not the result of over-zeal for His glory and the good of the House, although it frequently calls itself by that name, but it is a sheer temptation and danger to the spiritual life. It is as much a danger as that foolish, dreaming desire always to reach something better, even here on earth, which besets some characters. I do not mean, of course, the genuine desire to attain to virtue at no matter what cost to self, but the desire to "find", ready-made, something better than that which we have. It often manifests itself in Religious in a restless hankering after some other vocation or some other Order. If not quite so pronounced as that, then in a desire for change of work or change of position. Change, one notices, in their vocabulary is usually synonymous with ascent.

One may observe that such people, if they do change, nearly always end up *solus*. Even among the saints this has been the case, Benedict Labre for instance, and among very holy men we can number Charles de Foucauld. Actually they do not find what they are looking for—the perfect Order which is everything they desire. That is because the more we desire, the less likely we are to find it on this side of the grave.

Let us face the issue squarely and firmly. Our absolute ideal does not exist exteriorly on earth. But it exists in spirit, and we shall find it in our own individual spiritual life if we go on patiently putting up with the actuality which we have, and making the best of it. It is a very good best if we view it from the right angle and not from the dreaming heights of wishful thinking. Charity begins at home and so does perfection. The home inside each one of us: the home of God in which He promised that He would come and dwell with us.

To be half-hearted in the service of God, on the other hand, is to allow ourselves to fall into the folly of making not the best but the worst of both worlds. It is just sheer, heartbreaking waste: but not the glorious and intentional waste of sacrifice and libation. We shall usually find that real tepidity in the soul is reflected in increasing immortification. In the world, at all events, it is recognized that both food and sleep can be used almost as drugs—that is, that people who are unhappy will sleep and eat far more than is good for them, simply because these things have a deadening effect upon their sensibilities and emotions. That is an extreme case which, please God, does not and could not occur in Religion, but the tendency and its effects are nevertheless worth remembering.

I recollect so well a conversation three of us once had during the Christmas period, in our old Novitiate, when a little more talking is allowed. The room was hung rather limply with holly and evergreens which we had prepared in honour of the Novice-Mistress, but I doubt if any of us were very much in love with our decorative efforts. It is completely impossible to get an air of worldly festivity into what is, when all is said and done, not an occasion of worldly festivity, and personally I prefer a statue of the Infant Jesus of Prague in all His best vestments, with pearls and imitation jewels hung round His neck, and a lot of nice little candles round His feet, and the whole world grasped in His small left hand while He blesses us with His right—to anything in the shape of garlands. I am not good at garlands and, as far as I am concerned, the Novitiate can keep its holly and dead leaves and paper rosettes, and I am afraid I must have intimated as much because Sister Veronica, rather untactfully, began to talk about the devil.

I had not mentioned the devil and I did not think it was altogether nice of her to introduce him like that. The Professed Novice, who was helping us to beautify the scene, intervened with pleasant remarks, which again were quite unnecessary, but Sister Veronica clung obstinately to the Enemy.

"Why," she demanded, "when he comes up to one and says: 'Now you come along with me and we will take a little walk together,' does one immediately go off with him instead of saying . . ."

"Oh, but we don't," cried the Professed Sister, shocked.

"What ought we to say to him?" I enquired earnestly, dropping all the floppy chrysanthemums on the floor and finding a gleam of interest in the conversation at last.

"We ought to say to him 'Avaunt' or 'Get behind me, vile wretch', or something nice and sharp off the St. Benedict medal, or else take holy water, or . . ."

"Yes, holy water," said the Professed, relieved, and went and took some herself to give the good example.

"If only somebody would give one a strong nudge in the ribs and say, 'Look out, here he comes again', it might give one a chance. . . ."

"One's guardian angel . . ." suggested the Professed feebly.

"Not nearly as quick as the devil—at least mine isn't," said Sister Veronica, shaking her head.

"Perhaps," I suggested politely to the Professed, "like St. Ignatius you have an archangel, which would, of course, account for his greater speed."

"Oh, dear," murmured the Professed, "I wonder if I had better fetch the Novice-Mistress. . . ."

"Quick," I cried under my breath, "chrysanthemums—trailing things—gold paper—anything——" We waved all the treasures of the wet garden in her face and between us got her interested again in the statue of the Little Flower. As we placed wobbly tissue roses at her feet I thought the saint had a slight but understanding pucker at the corner of her mouth and I began to feel better.

"Avaunt," I said, quite firmly.

"Get thee behind me—never will I listen to thy suggestions," chorused Sister Veronica.

"Wicked fiend, return whence thou camest and leave me alone where I have come . . ." I echoed, getting positively buoyed up.

"That's the end of him for to-day," said Sister Veronica with satisfaction, throwing holy water in all directions, even over the Professed.

"You two," began the latter, wiping the drops off her best veil, "really . . ."

I do not know how Sister Veronica got to see it in after years, because she went to God soon after profession and found out all these things for herself, but without being able to tell me; but it did not take me so very long to discover that one of the reasons why we do listen is because it does not sound like the devil: it sounds like ourselves reasoning, and reasoning very well. Just so was Eve tempted: she could not believe that that kind and intelligent creature was the devil.

Now it is, of course, possible that, on any given occasion, it really may be ourselves and that we *are* being sensible; but if we had made up our minds to a certain course which seemed good to us (and others), or against a certain course which seemed bad to us (and others): or even if it is merely a case of something contrary to what is generally considered the good and Christian and supernatural course—let us be very certain that it *is* us before we adopt the suggestion. The devil is a very clever impersonator.

First, is the suggestion to something better, easier, happier, and apparently more worth while than the course we had decided upon? Then let us beware. The devil is not such a fool as to tempt to something harder—only God dares do that. God dares because He knows that He has the grace to give which goes with the need for it; the devil is not such a fool as to tempt to something harder because he knows that he has no grace to give, and so can only offer something apparently easy, something pleasant, something which he knows we can accomplish unaided, or with no more than the aid of the world, the flesh and himself.

Is it something which will harm another in even the slightest degree? Although we may tell ourselves that it is our duty—only right—for the ultimate good of all? Then let us beware. The devil never tempts to charity. Only God does that, because God Himself is love. Turning a blind eye to the faults of others; that is a temptation of God and we may safely fall into it.

Does it involve haste of any sort? Then again beware: the devil has to be quick lest the soul becomes conscious of his snares before she is caught in them. Only God can afford to wait.

Let us ask ourselves quietly what we thought about all this yesterday, and see whether we can find any serious reason for a change of mind. Are we just inventing reasons for turning back from the higher path? Is this, in short, really us speaking, or are we merely repeating what the devil is whispering in our ear?

If we will not sit down and answer these questions soberly, then we may be sure, without more questioning, that it is the devil. In that case there is only one thing to be done. To turn short round with an abrupt "No, no, no." A firm stand made at the beginning saves hours of subsequent misery and doubt: saves a bad conscience: saves ultimate humiliation and apologies in all directions: above all, saves that miserable sense of being no longer friends with Our Lord. For we cannot walk with one hand in His and the other clasping that of the devil; that is sure.

There are souls in Religion who have to fight these sort of recurring temptations all their lives, but are none the worse Religious for that. To those watching, it may look like a case of tightrope-walking, but God has them by the hand. It would be a queer thing perhaps to arrive in Heaven on the end of a tightrope but, after all, it does not matter so much how one gets there, so long as one arrives.

2 p.m.

VESPERS—AND AN ENCLOSURE WALL

THE bell is ringing to call us to Vespers, the most important and solemn office of the day—which indeed it is meant fittingly to close. That we should appear to be anxious to close ours somewhat early is not altogether our fault. Originally this office was called the "Evening Hour" (or *Vespertina synaxis*), and was celebrated with many lights and much pomp; but that was before the sixth century, about which period St. Benedict introduced some changes in its construction, in that he advanced the time of it to the hour of sunset, so that it was said before there was any need for artificial light, somewhere between four and six p.m. according to the season.

I always feel it is a little unreasonable of him to object to the time at which Carmelites say it, when it was he himself who first made a change; but of course I never mention that out loud, and in any case we get right again with Complin which we say at the hour at which it was meant to be said. Complin is the office which St. Benedict introduced as the actual " Evening Hour " with reference to time, thus effecting a kind of " doubling " of the original office of *Vespertina* or *Lucernarium*. The main point in life, after all, is to begin and end right, and that we do with Prime at 6 a.m. and Complin at 7.40 p.m.

The first mention of the office of Vespers as we know it to-day is somewhere about the year 530, and since then it has scarcely changed at all, for it was composed from the first of four psalms (now five), a chapter (capitulum), hymn, canticle (now invariably the Magnificat), prayers and litany. In the very earliest days of all, Lucernarium was the evening office corresponding as to time with our Complin (or thereabouts) and as to construction with our present-day Vespers. Just as Vigils (now Matins and Lauds) was the most solemn office of the night, so it was of the day, and consisted of many psalms as well as lessons and appropriate prayers.

There is nothing so lovely in the religious life as the sense of continuity—of belonging to something big and ancient—something which has lasted for centuries and will last on until the end of Time.

The May sun is warm and golden as we come out of choir at the end of Vespers, and the garden seems the obvious place in which to spend the half-hour of prayer or spiritual reading which follows. Prayer and spiritual reading : where does one end and the other begin? I never know, and so find that the best thing is to mix them happily together, for whilst one can be sure when praying with closed eyes that one is not

D

reading, who could be sure when they were reading that they were not also praying? To-day, in any case, I am doing neither, for the Novices have set me thinking, and what I am thinking about—without deluding myself into calling it "meditation"—is religious vocations in general, and how they come to be lost and how they come to be saved.

This is a subject which I believe we, as Religious, ought to think more about: those who have ever had the temptation to lose theirs, in order to avoid the catastrophe, and those who, by the mercy of God, have never had that temptation, in order to be the more kindly and understanding to those who have. For there is no escaping that some do, and that some even give way to it, and it is no sort of help to say, "Dear, Dear!" and look shocked and shake one's head after they have crept, or leapt, miserably back to a forlorn world where—whatever they think when they forsake us—we who are left behind know quite well they will never again find that happiness which is ours, and was once theirs: even were it only the suffering, courageous, self-sacrificing happiness which, so long as they stay where God put them, remains with them to the end of life, and which is not worth bartering for all the wealth and excitement and gratifications of the world. (Even, that is, if they get them, which mostly they do not. All they get is the cold, or shall we say lukewarm, shoulder of half-pitying, half-disedified relations and friends, and the possible applause of the passing crowd whom they neither know nor care for.)

> Just for a handful of silver he left us,
> Just for a riband to stick in his coat,
>
> .   .   .   .
>
> We shall march prospering—not thro' his presence,
> Songs may inspirit us—not from his lyre;
> Deeds will be done—while he boasts his quiescence,
> Still bidding crouch whom the rest bade aspire.

All the same we must be quite clear upon one point.   At

VESPERS—AND AN ENCLOSURE WALL   51

a certain stage in the Middle Ages it was sometimes thought,
and taught, that a man (or woman) who lost his vocation, or
refused to follow his vocation, also lost his soul. That is not
the teaching of the Church to-day. A vocation is an invita-
tion, an opportunity, a grace, a miracle if you like, but, even
when lost, it is not, and cannot be in itself, a cause of damna-
tion. It can, however, be a tragedy, because a vocation to
anything directly to do with God and with Religion, is a call
to something out of the ordinary, a little higher than the
ordinary, and if we deliberately forsake it and return to the
ordinary, we have lost just that something extra, in life and
in eternity, which was offered us.

We have not, please God, lost our souls, unless we are so
foolish as to fall into despair at our own folly and cast God
out of our hearts; but we have lost an unique, an irreplaceable
grace, and we have lost it in a particularly foolish manner.
We have lost it, that is to say, not by genuinely missing it
through stupidity and carelessness, not by any want of perception on our part, but by a single, concentrated, graceless
and ungrateful act—that of throwing back God's gift in His
face and saying we do not want it.

I look at the sunny garden wall, above which the thrushes
are singing so gaily, and the ghost of a fear grips my own
heart. So short a distance between this garden and the world
beyond, and only the grace of God and two feet of brick to
separate us from it. Well, the grace of God is sufficient.

But the little grey ghost is still there: the ghost of a companion I once had in the Novitiate. She drifted away after
profession and then, one day, some time later, came back
to see me in the parlour. She was something the same, yet
curiously different; but the soul which looked at me through
her eyes was the soul of the sister I had once known.

We talked quite simply about it all, and as I listened I knew
that it could have been averted; that she herself could have
averted it. I think she knew that too although she did not
actually say so. She had even made a tentative effort at
return—on paper—she told me: but again I think we both

knew that, at that stage, it would have been no good. The end of the half-hour came and she stood up to go.

"You're just the same," she said, "thank you for seeing me." There was, after all, I reflected, no reason why I should be any different. I had no answer and we stared at each other for a moment in silence. She went to the door; then came back. Her eyes searched my face as if for a clue to my feelings. Our glance met in the old friendly sympathy of long-dead days. She held the iron spikes, turned now against her, in her two hands as she leaned forward. Then:

"I just wanted to tell you, so that you'd know for sure: outside of Religion there is no meaning in anything else for us; it is all dust and ashes . . . dust and ashes. . . ." She was gone before I could reply.

Religious, I reflected, still staring at the ridge of blue above the wall where the lime-blossom is drenching the air with its scent, should be the first to try and find out the cause of these occasional defections. They concern only a small proportion it is true, but that proportion is not quite so small as it appears because, as a matter of fact, there are cases of precisely the same kind where the Sister does *not* leave the cloister but remains within it, to turn ultimately into a tragedy primarily for herself and secondly, in some degree, for her community. This latter is of no great importance, and indeed one of the modern French foundresses is reported to have said that if a community had not at least one difficult Sister, they would have to send out and buy one. Personally I would rather spend the money on something more useful, but in any case it is not so much the effect on the community which has to be considered as the effect on the Sister herself.

It is not easy to arrive at any general cause of such troubles but at least one can set on one side some of the things which might be but are not.

It is not likely in reality—though often in fiction—to be due to a mistake in originally accepting the vocation, because one must assume that such an obvious mistake as that would have become noticeable to the community in general long before profession. It is surely fantastic to suppose that such a blunder would not soon be detected either by the Superior who had made it, or the Sister who had asked for it to be made, or the chapter who had assented to its being made.

It is something surely which happens in the Religious herself, but which need not happen. It is a *result* of something, and is not present when the Sister enters, nor even for some time after. It is also something which grows : which makes one think that it could be checked if caught at the right point. It is not a case of certain types which are unsuitable. Undoubtedly there are such types, but the fact becomes apparent almost at once.

One cannot help wondering if it is not something of which we all carry the possibility within us, and which could develop in all of us. Where, then, do these particular Religious manage to go wrong? Obviously it is not, and cannot be, God who is to blame. It cannot altogether be the community, unless of course it could be definitely proved that the Sister in question had been urged to stay against her will—again something which only happens in fiction and not in fact, and has its origin in the imagination of those who have never tried a Novitiate themselves. If she had not wanted the community, or the community had not wanted her, the situation would have come to a head long before four and a half years—the shortest period before which the final step can be taken.

So we come to this : that it is something which develops later : not God : not the community. Then self? That is all which is left except the devil. So one is forced to the conclusion that it is just that : self. If a Religious has not really given everything to God in the religious life, disaster follows : everything, that is, according to individual capacity and circumstances which, needless to say, vary very greatly. Nine out of ten Religious do give it, or at least near enough to satisfy a merciful God : the tenth does not. That is all.

Yet they must have meant to give it or again it would have been noticed. They meant to, or they themselves would have been unhappy earlier, as they are now unhappy, because they are living a life in which they ought to be giving everything to God, and they know that they are not.

The fact is indisputable : if you are giving everything to God in the religious life you are inevitably happy. You are happy because that gift of self carries with it the return of the gift of God to the soul (God never allows Himself to be outdone in generosity, said St. Teresa of Avila) and that gift of God contains within it all the peace, the quiet happiness of complete trust, which the world does not know and consequently cannot assess. "The peace of God which passeth all understanding." All this, of course, is in exact relationship with the spiritual capacity of each individual : not the capacity of the saints no doubt : but, again, the capacity of any particular Religious cannot have been too hopelessly inadequate or it would have been noticed in earlier days.

It is always assumed that the question of vocation is an entirely individual question at all stages, and so of course in a certain sense it is. Nevertheless there are recognized general spiritual rules, and rules of perfection, which all of us have to accept, and outside of which we go wrong in the spiritual and religious life. Individual Sisters may come to feel that they have after all made a mistake, that this is not their vocation, that they were called to something else or not called at all. Naturally this only applies to professed Religious, for before profession there is obviously no reason whatsoever why a Novice, or a Superior, should not discover a genuine mistake : but again, I say to myself, such genuine mistakes are exceedingly rare. Those who are already professed must surely realize that such a step is not undertaken lightly. Both they and their religious Superior considered that a vocation to their own particular Order did, in fact, exist at the moment when they took their vows, and those vows were their own formal acceptance of the vocation.

Once again, I have to remind myself that there is no actual sin involved in giving up a vocation, provided proper dispensations can be procured, but the tragedy of giving up, or the tragedy of going on while inwardly wishing that one could give up, is what one would do anything to avert.

As long as the problem is treated in each case as a purely individual problem, with the Religious asserting that she never had a vocation to *this*, and the Superior assuring her that she undoubtedly had, the result is almost a foregone conclusion, for it is difficult to persuade such sufferers that, in their own particular, individual case, they do not know best.

Suffering, after all, however misguided, is suffering, and agony of soul is agony. And such people really can suffer genuine agony. It is easy enough to say that it need not be, that it is their own fault, and that personally one would never feel like that. Perhaps one would not. It may all be perfectly true, but the fact still remains that agony is agony even when it is unreasonable, and that such a frame of mind can be agony.

In *The Sign of Jonas* Thomas Merton deals with just such a problem, but I do not know that he gives the universal answer.

"I soon came to the conclusion that I could not think straight about the problem anyway. Perhaps this is not the most perfect vocation in the Church, *per se*. . . . It seems to be *my* vocation. That is the thing that matters. . . . But how can it be my vocation if I have such a strong desire for some other vocation? Don't ask me. Our Lord wants that sacrifice. How do I know? I don't know. That is what I am told. Do I have to believe them? I do not have to I suppose . . . but . . . my conscience is on the side of my Superiors, and anyway, when I have a moment of lucid thought on the subject, experience reminds me that these feelings will go away just as they have gone away before. I was Thurifer at the Solemn Abbatial Mass of reposition. On top of all my other troubles. I could not get a decent fire going. . . ."[1] He wouldn't. Any of us could have told him that. One never does get anything decent going under such circumstances.

[1] *The Sign of Jonas*, Thomas Merton, p. 23-24.

Even after Solemn Profession, although much surer, he does not yet seem quite sure. "Just because a cross is a cross, does it follow that it is the cross God intends for you? Just because a job is a nuisance, is it therefore good for you? Does the fact that all this is obedience make it really pleasing to God? I wonder. I do not ask these questions in a spirit of rebellion. I would really like to know the answers."[1]

One feels so confident that there never was any real rebellion in Thomas Merton, and that he really did want the answers as so many of us have perhaps wanted them, that one is not surprised that he got them all, long before even the end of his own book. All the same, generally speaking, those questions should not really have to be asked after Solemn Profession for the simple reason that not everyone is a Thomas Merton, and there is just the possibility that they may never get the right answers. That, in fact, is precisely what causes the tragedies of which I am sitting in the garden and thinking, on such a lovely May afternoon that it does not seem possible that there could ever be a spiritual tragedy in the world, let alone behind an enclosure wall.

We must remember however that not even every Religious conscience is on the side of its Superiors by any means, and it is for those very consciences which are not that it is so important to have some general line of thought to guide them, other than the intensely individual line of thought which they usually follow, and which only lands them in the same old quagmire of personal doubt. Of rules there are none, one need hardly say, but there may be certain sensible ways of thinking.

Let us try to absorb a little of the idea of finality, of stability, of fulfilment. Actually, with final profession, our vocation is accomplished. It was a vocation to the religious life, and here we are, finally and irrevocably engaged in the religious life. We have responded to our call: as far as that went we have fulfilled it. What then remains? The grace of God never ceases and God's action on our souls is continuous.

[1] *The Sign of Jonas*, Thomas Merton, p. 44.

He did not promise that, if we answered His first call, He would never ask us anything again, never urge us afresh to something better. Religious life is progressive just as every other life is progressive—or retrogressive.

We get further calls from God as life goes by—what else could we expect?—calls to a humility, a patience, a self-surrender, such as probably we did not dream of when we entered Religion. It is to these that God now invites us, calls us just as He called us in those first blessed days when we accepted and undertook the initial stages of the spiritual and religious life. And it is to this later vocation that we are failing to respond. We are tired : we thought we had already arrived : we had not bargained for anything more—certainly not for *this* sort of thing. And so, turning our backs and looking wistfully towards the land which we have long since left, we begin to plead that we were never called to leave it at all.

The truth is that we are cowards; that is all that is wrong with us, and wrong with our vocation. It was and is a vocation to courage and, because we are failing in it and wish to hide our own defeat, we try to persuade ourselves that it is our past and not our present which is wrong. If our past were wrong, that alone could justify us now, in our own eyes at least, in making such havoc of our to-day and to-morrow.

We are utterly and unequivocally mistaken. If we had never had the vocation, we should have found it out long before this. If we had never had the vocation, those responsible for us and those having to live with us would have found it out long before this. If we had never had the vocation, *God* would have known it always, and He would never have given us the grace to answer His call then, and to pledge ourselves solemnly, as we have done, to answer it to the end of our lives. To say that we have done all this without the grace of God is such a manifest absurdity that it needs no reply. Does God offer His grace to follow a call which He had never given and never meant? What are we trying to make of God in our efforts to escape from the tangle of our own cowardice?

What is tripping us up now is either some fresh demand upon our courage and constancy, or some fresh sacrifice of our pride and self-will. Either we find ourselves faced with something which we do not want to do, or faced with the loss of something which we had wanted and now realize that we are never going to get. We must remember that there is many a secret ambition (perhaps even secret from ourselves) which we may almost unconsciously have cherished as a part of our projected religious life, but which, until now, has never tripped us up for the simple reason that it was something which we subconsciously knew must be relegated to the maturer years which lay beyond.

In due course maturity comes, and with it the knowledge, seeping slowly and almost unnoticed into the mind that, after all, that piece of work, that opportunity, that particular grace, whatever it was, does not seem to be God's will for us. Perhaps the knowledge comes gradually, disintegrating our resistance before we have realized it; or maybe it comes with some sudden merciless crash which we feel that we cannot survive. These are rare cases, certainly, still they do occur; and even if they only occur once in fifteen or twenty years, that remains once too often.

But going back will never help us—still less will it justify us. For past steps in life can never be retraced so exactly that they are, as it were, obliterated by the retracing. The most that we can do, turning our backs upon the scene of our defeat, which might have been the scene of our surpassing victory, is to leave behind us a second and more wavering line of fleeing footprints, indelibly engraved beside those first forward steps of our more gallant youth.

Meanwhile creaking doors can hang for ever—even until Eternity when they will creak no longer. There was a nun in France, not so very long ago, who struggled with difficulty all her religious life. Periodically a fresh opportunity in another Carmel, even in another country, was found for her. She wandered here and there, but always within some kindly enclosure, and always in her own confused way, a good Religious at heart. In between each fresh essay, her own original community received her back with unfailing love and patience. Finally she became ill—an operation was advised. At short notice she was rushed to the nearest hospital under nursing Sisters in another town. They were immensely edified by the resignation and virtue of the Carmelite; the operation was successful; then, as in so many cases of operation, she had to be told that she had but a few hours to live.

Her joy was extreme; lying back on her pillows with an expression which was a mixture of astonished incredulity and delight: "*Mais—après tout, j'ai été fidèle!*" she exclaimed.

The nursing nuns were mystified, but at that she left it and, beyond a message of love and gratitude to her Prioress, said no more until she said what she had to say to God. The Sisters wrote an account to her Carmel. They repeated with some emphasis the cryptic words: they had not understood what the good Sister could have meant, but they were quite sure that they were reporting them accurately. Her Prioress was quite sure too, and thanked God as she laid aside the letter happily enough.

"*Après tout*—dear Merciful Lord of us all—*après tout*—and who could believe it, knowing me?—*après tout*—in spite of the faltering, and the half-returns, in spite of the tears and the restlessness and the blind ingratitude—by your grace, dear pitiful God who created me—*après tout, j'ai été fidèle.*"

3 p.m.

"J'Y SUIS, J'Y RESTE"

THE best working time of the day for us lies between 3 and 5; an uninterrupted stretch of work in which one can really get something done. Not that this time need necessarily all be spent in doing the same thing, but at all events it is a stretch of uninterrupted work.

Cutting altar breads is surely an occupation which would have delighted the heart of St. Teresa of Avila—although the complication of the machine which cuts them might have astonished her considerably. Her spinning-wheel could scarcely have looked as shining and dapper as this although we, in company with her, work it by a treadle and our own energy, and not by electricity. If we cut crooked, we cut crooked, and no one can blame a failure of any current except their own current.

Cutting altar breads is the perfect work from the point of view of a Carmelite because, while it takes physical energy and great attention to what one is doing, yet it does really leave the mind free to meditate and to reflect. "The nuns are not to engage in very elaborate work, but in sewing and similar occupations, which are not of such a nature as to absorb the mind excessively and hinder the spirit of recollection", or, as the old rendering had it, "and prevent them from fixing the mind upon God". And then we come to what *is* the spirit of recollection, and what is fixing the mind upon God?

Some people feel, of course, that such purely manual work as this is not sufficiently engrossing for modern brains; but when all is said and done, brains have always been much the same, some profound and some shallow, some active and some sluggish. Rather monotonous mechanical work alone might indeed have a deadening effect on the mind of anyone; reflection alone might seem to some people to be a selfish and lazy way of spending long periods of time. But an hour or so spent with God which meanwhile results in boxes full of neatly cut altar breads—or anything else for the matter of that—is surely the perfect combination?

But then, how exactly is one to spend the time with God? Needless to say there are a dozen different ways, and each one will have his or her particular devotion, but in general the answer is surely to *be* with God: consciously, that is, with God.

I have a friend, a pedlar, who comes periodically to visit me in the parlour, and to tell me how business is doing, and all about the interesting people he meets. He loves his work, there is no doubt as to that, and always refers to it as his vocation. He regards it as very similar to mine, and he talks more to me about prayer than anything else. He tells me how he enjoys everything in company with Christ: the day's rain, the day's sunshine; the birds' nests in the hedges in the spring; the cattle being driven home across the fields in the light of the evening sun.

"Sometimes," he once added confidentially, "I can't even help saying it out loud: 'Oh, dear Lord, do look at that pretty red roof shining in the sun!' Do you think He minds my pointing out His own creation to Him like that?" And there is the answer to one's "how" in a nutshell.

I often think of the convert I once met in the world, who was seeking advice as to how to eat a bun to the glory of God. This she had been advised to do by her confessor because, we gathered, she was too fond of buns, but she had not the vaguest idea how to set about it; neither, apparently, had anyone else in the assembled company.

"Well, you just do it, you know," said the C.E.G. member, who felt that Catholic Evidence personnel ought always to be able to supply an answer to any doubt. "Eat it, you know —to the glory of God——"

"Well, I do eat it," agreed the convert, "but how do I include the glory of God?"

"You don't include the glory of God in the bun, but the bun in the glory of God," said the silent young man, and said no more. We thought it over.

"Would beginning with grace be sufficient?" enquired the convert at last weakly.

Most emphatically it would. So long as one remembers that God made the bun, or at all events permitted the bun, because He made the wheat of which it is composed; and put

the brains inside the head of the chef who first thought how
to mix and bake it; and gave us a palate wherewith to taste
it, and something inside us, although one is not quite sure
what, with which to digest it; as long as we remember all
that and thank Him for it, then we can safely eat buns to our
hearts' content, and they will do us no harm either spiritually
or otherwise.

There was also the postulant who had a brother for whom
she particularly wished to pray, and who was told to "make
that her intention". She came back after half an hour and
said that she had sat in choir and said "John, John, John,
John," over and over until she was giddy, and she did hope
that was all right, but all the same she was simply dead—
and there is no point in even repeating the things which she
said about intentions in general and John's in particular.

God created everything, and so long as we are thinking of
that Creation *in relation to its Creator*, we are surely in company with Him. Take colours, for instance. Going back to
the beginning of Nature, one can so easily find out the colours
which God loves. We have forced our colours, and
emphasized our colours, until we hardly know what pure
colour is.

But the colours which God chose for us to live amongst
were the green of young grass in the spring, and the green of
all the forest trees for our delight; even, if we are sad, the
softer, dustier green of olive trees to match our mood. The
rich and perfect blue of the sky, fringed in the evening with
mauve and rose and saffron, or the pale grey of driving clouds
across a winter landscape. The golden glory of sun in mid-
summer, or shafts of its pale yellow light falling across
autumn fields. The wonder of October woods, a dream of
grey and brown, russet and crimson, with great white clouds
and a reddening sky above.

Let those who want us to live for ever surrounded by the
glare of scarlet and orange and shrieking blues and greens,
sometimes pause to remember that God, after all, set us in a
world of softer shades, with the light of the sun artfully

diffused, and the silver shining of the moon set in a darker sky to frame its loveliness. Of the more violent colours there is only a temperate and occasional use : the last crimson rays of a sinking sun; the richness of ripe apples half hidden by clustering leaves; the passing radiance of a rose-pink dawn, or the angry violet of swift storm-clouds across a leaden sky. But in between God gave us for the most part the soft, gay shades of natural beauty which were His own setting for Man.

We have exaggerated in exactly the same way for both sound and perfume. There are probably not so many people nowadays to whom the clear trills of the song of a thrush are as real music, or who would stop for a moment to appreciate the delicate, illusive fragrance of a primrose, a cowslip, or a field of clover in the spring.

Those who, consciously or unconsciously, want to live in the world of God's and not man's creation, will find that most of their joy in life comes to them from within; from what is in their own mind, and what is reflected back into that mind from God and from His earth. This, however, is not just a refined form of egoism, nor is it introversion, that melancholy " turning towards his own inner self and the twilight world of the unconscious, the primordial images ", as W. P. Witcutt so depressingly calls it.[1]

It is true that most of their joy in life, which is great, comes to them through their own soul and mind, and but rarely from those around them or from purely external events—a fact which sometimes annoys other people who feel that, in a sense, they cannot reach them (or at all events cannot hold them), and equally annoys the devil who fails to obtain that sinister grip on them which he is accustomed to obtain through the passing events and accidents of life. But this is not due to egoism, introspection, or any of the modern developments of nervous and psychological disorders. It is, I reflect, a difficult thing to put into words, but it seems to arise from a certain directness of impression; from an absence of intermediaries between themselves and the world of God

[1] *Catholic Thought and Modern Psychology*, W. P. Witcutt, p. 24.

and of Nature, so that they draw their happiness and their energy direct from the original Source.

Where this attitude towards existence is firmly based upon God, it is indeed the first beginning of the grace of detachment, which sets me thinking again of the subject which I left behind me in the garden, that is the subject of religious vocation, and Religious in general. What quality, or combination of qualities, is it which makes a really good and happy Religious?

I suppose it could scarcely be one alone, but certainly there is one which is very much in favour of it, and that is this virtue of detachment, and one which is very greatly against it, and that is a critical spirit. Of all the things which ruin religious life, a critical spirit is surely the most pernicious. The critical faculty may be of great value in many walks of life : in the art of government; for obtaining perfection in the arts themselves; in business affairs; and even turned on our own conduct it has a certain usefulness, so long as it is not overdone and does not lead to discouragement and scruples. But in ordinary religious or home life, in the general spiritual and social life of individuals, to open the door to criticism is to open the door to unhappiness itself. "When poverty comes in at the door, love flies out of the window", is an old saying which is by no means always true, but it is perfectly safe to say that when criticism comes in at the door, Charity simply takes to its heels.

The nearer to God we are the further shall we be from criticism—other than that legitimate and constructive criticism which is always permissible. The reason is simple. The nearer we are to God, the more we become aware of His infinite beauty and perfection, and the more we become aware of our own utter lack of virtue. That is not a state of soul in which the spirit of criticism flourishes. On the contrary it has learnt to make allowances. It allows for human frailty and knows that the genuine effort after holiness, provided that it is really genuine and persevering, is what counts in the eyes of God. All the rest is the almost inevitable outcome of human weakness and, even more often, of human lack of vision.

To console ourselves there is always this to be said: if we could find perfection upon earth, it would not be perfection but an illusion on our part, for perfection belongs to Heaven. When it comes to detachment, that is so much a matter of grace that it is difficult to define it in any sort of practical way for the use of ordinary people, such as ourselves, who nevertheless really wish to acquire it. A very small test of whether we are anywhere within sight of it, is whether we can bear to separate the results of the things which we do completely from the person who did them: ourselves?

As a small step in the right direction, for instance, if we do something either for love of God or our neighbour, and it is not in any way attributed to us—can we take it cheerfully? (A saint, of course, would not even be aware of the omission.) Another longer step in the same direction would be if it were attributed not to us but to someone else, and remained attributed to them: can we take that cheerfully? If so, there is hope. After all, if we do a charity and it is appreciated and well received, so far so good no doubt, but it was not exactly the way in which our Lord's redemption of us was appreciated and regarded, was it? It was not the way in which the Apostles and their work were regarded: they were for the most part martyred.

Our most perfect charity is the one entailing sacrifice and generosity which are never recognized. That is the authentic charity of Christ and therefore of the Christian—but it is not a particularly easy charity to practise, nor is it meant to be. Ingratitude in itself may be something detestable, but ingratitude applied to ourselves, or merely a lack of perception applied to ourselves, is a secret grace and treasure which one day we shall know how to appreciate.

There is still another tentative forward step which we can take of ourselves, and that is to give up just one (what seems to us) really big thing: something we deeply care about:

E

something which is almost a general principle with us : not a personal principle, for those can never be safely relinquished. Let us see if we can give it up completely for love of God. If anyone asks how, one can only suggest that the interior gesture is as if one opened one's hands and let something gently drop to the ground : no effort, no doing violence of any kind : just a quiet, unostentatious relinquishment.

For the rest, detachment—which is really almost the Alpha and Omega of a good Religious—is not a conscious effort after piecemeal virtues, but a slow transformation of the soul by the grace of God. The point of view changes. The virtue is unperceived because, if it exists, it exists as the result of that point of view, which again is the result of grace. These things being interior are almost entirely imperceptible in their action. We see the results but not the process. The persons concerned often do not even perceive the results (or only occasionally with some little shock of surprise and discovery) because the results are so bound up with the process as to be indistinguishable.

"If I see it like that, I *must* behave like that." So they behave like that, but they do not regard it as any particular exhibition of virtue. For, in the end, grace acts as a sort of Code. They almost, as one might say, cannot fall below it. Even if the conduct required is selfless, is crucifying, for them there is no alternative to the Code. It is, of course, always possible to lose grace—however long and however apparently perfectly acquired is the habit of using it—but, short of falling away from grace, they will behave according to their supernatural Code as they see it. A vision of perfection and love not given to most of us.

"This force we call grace," says Dr. Van Doornik,[1] " because without it the real conversion will never follow. Unaided personal effort can never lead you to a supernatural Credo. And neither can it lead you to the practice of supernatural virtues."

[1] *The Triptych of the Kingdom*, Van Doornik, p. 115.

Take saints, for instance: how unconscious they are of the height of their own practice of virtue! If canonized saints are too high for your imitation, take a modern monk, and a modern writer, who tells us so appealingly and so vividly of his own difficulties and his own ascent.

"The man who began this Journal is dead, just as the man who finished *Elected Silence* when this Journal began was also dead. . . . And now that all these men are dead . . . I think I will have ended up by forgetting them."[1] Dead, yes. But he does not say that he killed them. They just *died*, and each time a new Thomas Merton was born.

When one reads a book by any Religious really striving after God and perfection, an autobiographical book, that is, one cannot but notice the calmness with which they refer to sanctity and its attainment. It would be simply incredible to suppose that this arose from any want of humility on their part. Take St. Thérèse of Lisieux as an example—take Thomas Merton, who is in some way doing the same thing for religious life and the world now, as she did for religious life and the world of her day: bringing, that is, the two together.

She says placidly, " *Je ne sais pas si je suis sainte,*" whereas most of the rest of us, in our own case, are quite definitely assured upon the point. He also tells us how he dreamt that he was confiding to several monks that he would be a saint, and they did not seem to question him. Most of us are too sadly aware of the type of answer—not question—we should get to any such statements as to risk them with our own communities. "If I do become one—(I shall)——"[2] he adds cheerfully, and this time he is awake.

The fact is, of course, that they mean one thing by saint and we usually mean another. They mean the Biblical sort of saint which St. Paul tells us we are all called to be, whereas we mean that spectacular thing which gets itself canonized. That they do eventually turn from one into the

---

[1] *The Sign of Jonas*, Thomas Merton, p. 320.
[2] *The Sign of Jonas*, Thomas Merton, p. 315.

other is no part of their scheme for themselves, but only a part of ours for them, and they must not be blamed for it. They are thinking of sanctity in relation to God; it is we who think of it in relation to men and that is no fault of theirs.

Thomas Merton, who begins by having the same sort of difficulties as young Religious of every generation, only rather more so, ends by giving us a perfect picture of the happy and fervent Religious which it is not given to all of us to become. But we *could* all become it—in our degree. And if one is a fervent and happy Religious, or fervent and happy anything else, up to the limit of one's own particular spiritual capacity, God asks no more, and neither should we.

He begins with one of his characteristically encouraging remarks: encouraging, that is, to the rest of us. "Like the prophet Jonas, whom God ordered to go to Nineveh, I found myself with an almost uncontrollable desire to go in the opposite direction. God pointed one way and all my 'ideals' pointed in the other."[1] Later on he sets down the even more consoling reflection: "It is not much fun to live the spiritual life with the spiritual equipment of an artist." It is not. "It is not complicated to live the spiritual life," he adds thoughtfully, "but it is difficult. We are blind and subject to a thousand illusions. We must expect to be making mistakes almost all the time."[2] It is good indeed to hear that from one who all his life has made so many other and better things than mistakes.

But, as he gets through his beginnings, there follows what one might call the singing period. There is the old disused barn up into which he so loved to climb: "Where are you, O my God? I was ashamed of singing on the road to the barn, but what else could I have done? . . . The mud of my feet going up is the mud of my hands coming down. . . ."[3] And there is a good deal more in that last sentence than

[1] *The Sign of Jonas*, Thomas Merton, p. 8.
[2] *The Sign of Jonas*, Thomas Merton, p. 235.
[3] *The Sign of Jonas*, Thomas Merton, p. 318.

actually meets the eye. It is worth a considerable meditation all to itself.

And so we come finally to the perfected Religious. "I listen to the clock tick. Downstairs the thermostat has just stopped humming. God is in this room, so much so that it is difficult to read or write. . . . It is very quiet, O my God, Your moon shines on our hills. Your moonlight shines into my wide-open soul when everything is silent."[1]

"It is as if I were beginning all over again to be a Cistercian: but this time I am doing it without asking myself the abstract questions which are the luxury and the torment of one's monastic adolescence. For now I am a grown-up monk and have no time for anything but the essentials. The only essential is not an idea or an ideal: it is God Himself, who cannot be found by weighing the present against the future or the past, but only by sinking into the heart of the present as it is."[2]

4.30 p.m.

"LET THE WORK BE MANUAL"

OUT in the garden a blackbird is calling as I pack away the last of the altar-breads into the open tin. An hour or so spent with Our Lord, and an hour or so spent in helping, however humbly, to bring that same Lord to thousands of the Faithful in the Blessed Sacrament.

No one will ever make me quarrel with a Carmelite's way of spending her worktime, however disgruntled may be the comments of an intellectual world upon the subject. "Let

---

[1] *The Sign of Jonas*, Thomas Merton, p. 240.
[2] *The Sign of Jonas*, Thomas Merton, p. 321.

them as 'as 'em, gnash 'em," as the old lady said coming out of church after a sermon full of "weeping and gnashing of teeth". "Let them as 'as 'em, gnash 'em", and let those who are so intent on brains use them, in whatever way they prefer, out in the world: for the rest, we use our fingers, and toes as well, in the service of the Lord, and very happy it makes us.

If one were not cutting altar-breads then one would be either cooking, or counting, or packing them, for where a weekly output is anything from 80,000 to 100,000 breads, a good deal of work is necessarily involved. If one were not doing anything in connection with altar-breads, then one would probably be trying, not too successfully, to paint little sprays of roses on small cards with a picture of Baby Jesus attached, just to remind people next Christmas that the 25th December is primarily His Birthday and not a public holiday *per se*; or embroidering a panel of satin to go on a vestment in which some priest will ultimately dispense Our Lord in the Blessed Sacrament; or darning some other priest's torn alb so that it does not show for next Sunday's High Mass.

It is all one to an enclosed Religious so long as she is not asked to talk while she does it, nor to be interested in the business side of the arrangement. She does these things for love of our Lord, and she wants to listen to our Lord and to talk to our Lord while she does them, and she does not want to talk or to listen to anyone else. If a postulant did not feel like that about it after a few months inside the enclosure, my own personal advice to her would be to go home: but I imagine that under such circumstances she would probably go home in any case without waiting for my advice.

In the orchard there is a fallen tree still waiting to be sawn up into logs. Carmelites use old-fashioned means of heating —when they do heat, which is seldom—and whatever Sister Rose's feelings about my landscape gardening, she invariably beams at a pile of neatly cut-up wood. Sawing is a thing we used to do down in Devon, quite a little while ago now, and the smell of the logs, apple and pine and young green oak, still seems to rise and drift across the orchard as I get to work upon the more prosaic poplar and sycamore of our garden.

One used to be able to tell what logs were burning with one's eyes shut, just by the scent, or even more easily by the colour of the flame—green, blue, violet and rose-pink—or the vivid shoots of multi-coloured light from great lumps of dead sea-driftwood. Well, there is still the same blue and faintly pink sky of a late May afternoon; the same pale, perfect blossom on the orchard trees; and only the difference between the fragile evanescent happiness of youth, and the full-flowered happiness of maturity, to mark the passage of the years between.

It is an interesting point, that point about doing things for God instead of doing them for oneself or other people, even if it is precisely the same things which one is doing. If we are doing something for self, and we get tired of it, we very naturally stop. If we are doing something for creatures, and they change in any way towards us, we usually change too. If we are doing something for a purpose, and that purpose goes awry, we stop absolutely dead. In each case we hesitate or stop because our relationship with ourselves, or with people, or in regard to things, has been changed and upset, and that in turn changes and upsets us. We find that, for the moment at least, there is nothing to go on for.

But if we are doing something for God, and everyone and everything else changes, in so far as possible we still go on exactly as before, because God is the only one who never changes in His essential relationship to us, nor we in our essential relationship to Him. In a world the tide of which swirls and eddies unceasingly around us, nothing is changeless except Him. So, if it is for Him that we are acting, we find that in our own small degree we become changeless too, or as near changeless as is humanly possible, in regard to Himself.

That brings my thoughts to one of the most difficult moments in religious life for all concerned—a change of

Superior : for to us our Superior stands in the place of God, and therefore it is not always easy to see such a change in its right perspective.

In every Order, of course, the difficulty arises in a different degree, or even does not arise at all where the Superior is an Abbess and is elected for life. In many of the more modern Congregations also there is one Superior-General, and it is an understood thing that all the other Superiors can be moved from house to house according to the decisions of the General Chapter. In that case, from the first beginnng of religious life, it is known that Superiors do change, and that Religious do not remain permanently in any one convent, so that, although changes may often be deeply painful, at least they are neither rare nor unexpected.

Each Order or Congregation will know where its own shoe pinches, but there are certain general difficulties and adjustments which must necessarily be much the same in every case, and much the same virtue will be needed to meet them.

There is a nasty knot in the trunk of the old poplar which blew down in last autumn's storm but, having negotiated it, my thoughts go back again to the sort of virtues which are needed; because it is just as well to cultivate them in between whiles, and not to leave them to sprout of themselves at the last minute when they are urgently required and do not seem altogether inclined to rise to the occasion.

Such changes are really only opportunities for practising a little virtue and, if in the enclosed Orders which do not have Superiors for life, they seem at times hard, it is, between you and me, mostly for the very prosaic and even trivial reason that *habit* is being disturbed. Habit and routine are things which have to be guarded against in all enclosed Orders (regularity is quite another matter and has nothing to do with either) and from the point of view of virtue, nothing could be more salutary than a sudden, sweeping change in everyday life, in our emotions, in our occupations, and in our practical (needless to remark not spiritual) point of view. But to say that a thing is salutary is not to say that it is pleasant, and some may even be found to contend that any such disruption is bad in itself because it upsets contemplative prayer.

The answer to that is very short and very simple. Nothing should upset contemplative prayer except such a noisy confusion, such a bustling activity, such a preoccupation with mundane affairs that it becomes literally impossible to practise it. But trial should never interfere with real contemplative prayer, and indeed should rather increase its intensity since, in a time of trial, it is instinctively to our Lover that we turn for consolation and support. If contemplation is going to shrivel and die in our soul simply because we are faced with something which we do not like, then it has never been the contemplation of God, but only the illusory contemplation of something else : most likely of a reflection of ourselves.

"So that's that," say I to myself, and notice once more how pretty the apple-blossom looks against a sky now touching the edge of earth in lovely layers of green and pale yellow and smoky grey, as the sun rides down towards it.

It is quite true that, as a whole, a community should not think too much in terms of Superiors, except where each member's own individual obedience and loyalty are concerned. Nevertheless a community which never thinks of its Superiors in terms of the general difficulties and fatigues of that office may become a very selfish community, and, the more unselfish the Superior, the greater the danger.

As regards the actual change itself, there are obviously three points of view to be taken into account, although there is only one thing to be viewed, and that is the glory of God and His will; but—and that is the crux of the difficulty if difficulty there is—that glory and that will viewed from different angles. A humble, supernatural approach from every side will get everyone safely over any little jolts and jars from the very beginning. In the matter of unselfishness, there is not likely to be any shortage of it on the part of the two Superiors, for one will have been thinking of the good of others to the complete exclusion of her own for years, and the other will surely be the kind of Religious prepared to do the same, or we may be sure she would never have been chosen. Egoism is not an attractive quality, or one that endears in any walk of life, and the religious life is no exception.

The saw needs a little oil and I pause to apply it, but my thoughts run on uninterruptedly. There is so much to be thought, and so much to be left unthought; so much to be discarded and so much to be embraced; so much to do and so very much to leave undone in this matter, that perhaps the less thought about it the better. It is just one of the unexpected trials of religious life which have to be lived through, and probably the only one of the three concerned who can honestly meet it with a profound, although dutifully concealed, happiness and relief—since too blatant a joy might wound the feelings of a sensitive community—is the Superior going out of office.

Still, I reflect, even she must have her moments of difficulty just because of that tiresome thing called habit. Everything is necessarily changed for her except her actual environment, and the very sameness of the environment makes the changing of the habit more difficult. Her seat in choir, her seat in the refectory, the particular room in which she did most of her work and the cell where she slept, are all different. Where she went first as a matter of course, she now draws back; where she drew back, she now goes first. Where she spoke she is now silent; where she remained silent, she now speaks. Whenever we cease any accustomed occupation abruptly, there must almost inevitably be a sensation as of a pendulum swinging to and fro without for the moment anything in particular to swing for.

The remedy for any situation of this kind is probably the same wherever we find ourselves: to keep to the perfectly ordinary in so far as that is possible, seeing that the perfectly ordinary has suddenly been snatched away from us; to follow as usual any accustomed occupations that are left to us; above all, to pick up the new life without pause or gap and with the greatest possible interest. Life is not composed of one thing only, however congenial it may have been, and we must be very limited people indeed if we cannot accept some new turn in our existence. In the case of Superiors, the one all-important thing to be avoided is the faintest shadow or suspicion of any kind of lingering "power behind the throne". I am instantly ashamed that such a thought should even cross my mind, since it is only earthly thrones which have powers behind them, other than that all-sustaining and unique power of God.

I always remember a story told me by a one-time prioress. When she was a small child at school they used to sing a well-known song of that day:

> *Au clair de la lune*
> *Mon ami Pierrot,*
> *Prête-moi ta plume*
> *Pour écrire un mot.*
>
> *Ma bougie est morte,*
> *Je n'ai pas de feu,*
> *Ouvre-moi ta porte*
> *Pour l'amour de Dieu.*[1]

She said that it was not until years later, after a rather long term as Superior, that she really got the feeling of those verses. To give up office for her had been the really golden opportunity of her life to practise her vow of poverty. When she had left the world she had accepted in its place the poverty of the cloister, above all, poverty of desire and will: never a thing there when she wanted it—always a permission to be obtained. But a Superior, she explained, goes back temporarily, and whether she will or no, to something of the possessiveness of the world, in the sense that it is she who

[1] By the light of the moon   My candle's burnt out,
O, Pierrot, my friend,   I've no fire to rake,
Lend me your pen   Open your door
I've a letter to send.   For Christ's pitiful sake.

has, ultimately, to authorize the spending of her House and (within the strict limits of what is allowed by the Rule) she herself never actually lacks for anything essential, for the simple reason that it is somebody else's business to see that she does not.

She can, of course, take care to lack a great many things which she might have, and will never authorize the spending of a farthing of the community's money (and she has none of her own if she has Solemn Vows) upon herself exclusively, but only upon herself in common with all the other Sisters. Still, in comparison with the simple Religious, she is saved from that perpetual poverty-of-having-to-ask-permission which is perhaps the most conscious poverty of all, except the real poverty of indigence.

On relinquishing office, she told me, she had unexpectedly found what she considered the most priceless grace of her life. The renunciation had been made once before, but made blindly, scarcely knowing to what it was that she was pledging herself. Now she was given the chance to make it all over again, and this time with full consciousness. To go back and just be utterly poor, not only in intention but in fact: after spending, to have nothing to spend; after planning, to have nothing to plan; after providing, to be herself overlooked and unprovided for. "My dear child," she ended suddenly, with a genuine and delightful smile, "if there is one thing which makes it worth while spiritually to be Superior, it is to stop being it."

A sick Superior, she also suggested to me, might be the greatest possible grace for a community, provided that the sickness did not continue for too long. "It is the coming back to community life," she said, "that is so good for everyone; for her return is so different to these returns in the world; it is the return of the *whole person*. She may be a little thinner, a little paler perhaps, but the complete personality is there just as always. Most people, after a bad illness, crawl back in bits, with at least half of them missing for a time; but our Mother comes back to us just herself from the first moment. That is because," she added, "so much the larger part of her is her spirit which is quite untouched by the physical. So she comes back to us—her soul, with just enough flesh to wrap it in."

Too drastic changes are inclined to upset people's nerves, I reflected finally as I picked up the last bit of wood, but too drastic changes can easily be avoided. One has only to remember that planning is one thing but the carrying out of the plan is quite another. It does not take long to get an idea—think of an improvement—set people to work. But . . . what may give the hapless carriers-out an impression of tremendous fatigue is, not so much doing things in rapid succession, as beginning another thing before the first is finished. Going, that is, not from the end of one thing very quickly to another, which is on the whole exhilarating, but going from the *middle* of one thing to the next.

Overlapping does, as a matter of fact, induce a great sense of fatigue: of no pause, no respite. A quick mind arranges something; gives thought to the details; works it all out; then tells the various people concerned what they have to do. Now from her point of view, that is done with: finished: accomplished. She therefore puts it out of her mind and turns to the next thing, which in a quick and fertile brain will be in an exceedingly short time. She is apt to forget that other people are still struggling with the practical details of her previous vision. The people coming along behind her nearly expire in the endeavour to keep up, and the greater their goodwill the nearer they come to expiring.

In the world, of course, this does not matter at all, and indeed is an almost certain guarantee of success in an organizer, because it is possible to get a completely different set of workers on to the second plan, and the first are left to finish in peace. (Literally in peace, because the organizer is now mercifully busy with the second idea, praise be to God!) But in a religious community there is unfortunately only one community. . . .

The chickens are eating grass under the orchard trees as if

they were a herd of cows and, the sawing finished, I do my best to persuade them that they have had enough salad for one day and that it is now time to be shut up. They seem disinclined to agree, but as the preparation-bell for evening prayer begins to ring, I finally convince them, and together we make our way towards the house.

All the same, I reflect as an afterthought, if any government has been of the vigorous sort and one has become thoroughly used to it, it might be as well, should the next Superior be of the calm and deliberate type, not to slow down everything too abruptly. Brakes, suddenly applied, make a horrible noise, and a feeling of void is always demoralizing. A gentle relaxation is better perhaps than a sudden, awful hush.

I shoo the last of the chickens into their enclosure and at the same time round up my desultory thoughts towards a final conclusion:

If you have never been a Superior, thank God and pray that you never will be.

If you are a Superior, accept it with love of God and secret groanings of spirit, and pray for grace so long as the trial shall last.

If you have once been a Superior and no longer are, thank God with all your heart, and pray that you never will be again, and that you may not be judged too heavily for the days when you were.

These prayers should be prayed earnestly and with great sincerity each day by the appropriate Religious.

4.50 p.m.

PRAYER AND THE WAY OF IT

THE sun comes in at the choir windows just as it did early
this morning at Prime: but now it comes in from the west
instead of from the east, for our choir faces south. All a
day's work contained in that clear arc of the sun's journey
from dawn to setting, and of our day's journey through life.
That much time, which will never return to us, spent either
in the service of God or the service of self, in the service of
the neighbour or of our own interests.

In another ten minutes the bell will sound for prayer-time,
and we shall settle down to try to make some amends to God
for a day never spent well enough for the love He bears us;
never as fruitful as it might have been had we been different
and more faithful to that love; never as good measure as a
saintlier, more fervent soul would have pressed into it.

Since one is going to pray for an hour, it is surely worth
while to spend five minutes beforehand in trying to get a
clearer idea of precisely what it is that one is going to do, or
at least try to do. And the intention is always the first and
most important thing. For a contemplative Religious it is a
simple matter because her prayer is always the prayer of
intercession. That is her mission in the Church, that is the
whole purpose of her life. If she is not in her convent in
order to intercede for the world; for an earth which has tried
in some measure to withdraw itself from its Creator; for
sinners who have forgotten Him and His surpassing Love;
then she is in the convent under false pretences. Her whole
life is meant to be oriented towards that one desire, that one

goal: to make humble amends to God for all who turn from Him, wittingly or unwittingly; to draw down His pity and His mercy upon all who suffer and all who sin.

With that as her foundation, the contemplative nun prays as all others pray, and there are as many different ways as there are individual souls. There are, however, certain broad and generally recognized distinctions. Is one, for instance, going to pray aloud? Well, at this hour of the day, we at least are not. Is one going to meditate? Or is one going to try, as it were, to lose oneself in God, leaving the rest to Him? There is plenty of choice, but this latter prayer, which strictly speaking is the prayer of contemplation, is always at its safest when based upon the great crucial fact for us of Christ the Redeemer, Christ the Mediator, Christ the constant Friend of our earthly life.

"A saint," says Thomas Merton, "is not so much a man who realizes that he possesses virtues and sanctity, as one who is overwhelmed by the sanctity of God." So, at all events, let us too be overwhelmed by the sanctity of God, here at the beginning of our special hour with Him, even more than by the shame of our own laggard pursuit of holiness. "The contemplative life becomes awfully thin and drab if you go for several days at a time without thinking explicitly of the Passion of Christ, I do not mean necessarily meditating but attending with love and humility to Christ on the Cross."[1]

St. Teresa of Avila also said that, in her efforts to attain to pure contemplation, she tried for some time to avoid the thought of the humanity of Christ, but that ultimately our Lord Himself reproached her for this, and she was obliged to return to it. That is the basis of our prayer, the *point d'appui* from which we start and to which we always return at intervals: but in between lies much of prayer which is no longer meditation, but which Scaramelli calls an intellectual, experimental *knowledge* of God which begins with obscurity. "An interior something with which the soul is penetrated—

[1] *The Sign of Jonas*, Thomas Merton, p. 255.

a *sensation* of absorption, fusion, immersion."[1] This expression "spiritual sensation" is definitely used by him in order to draw our attention to a prayer other than that by way of thought.

Concerning this kind of prayer, Père Poulain noted, in an article written in the year 1893 for the *Messager du Coeur de Jesus* upon the Mysticism of St. John of the Cross, that mystical union, for which all contemplative prayer is in reality a preparation, has for its first characteristic that the presence of God is *felt*. The second characteristic, and the common basis of all the degrees of mystical union, is the fact that the spiritual impression by which God manifests His presence makes that presence felt in the way of an *interior* something by which the soul is penetrated. Thus it is clear that this form of prayer has nothing to do with visions or revelations, both of which are connected with created objects.

The further characteristics of this particular form of prayer are, among others, that it cannot be produced at will; that the knowledge of God received is obscure and confused, and is therefore sometimes described by such expressions as divine obscurity or darkness. Again, that it knows constant fluctuations, not retaining the same degree of intensity for five minutes together although, on the other hand, sometimes retaining the same *average* degree of intensity for quite a long time.

One point which he particularly mentions may well be a source of consolation to us : that the higher the degree of union the less effort is involved. So, whatever our way of praying, at least we need not strive for a sense of maximum output, thank God. I must confess that I have seen people whose foreheads were positively puckered with their efforts after the Prayer of Quiet. While not claiming any special knowledge of the Prayer of Quiet, simple common sense is sufficient to tell me that that, at all events, is not the way to get it.

When it comes to prayer, of course, a Carmelite must

[1] *Directoire Mystique*, Scaramelli. Tr. iii, no. 26.

F

always be inclined to return to the thought of St. Teresa and St. John of the Cross, and that particular point regarding effort is certainly very clearly emphasized in the case of the latter. Even in "The Dark Night of the Soul", though there is much of agony and spiritual pain, it is definitely never of his own creation, but the action of God, and his effort is confined to the effort of endurance; there is no straining what-soever after methods or results. It comes suddenly into my mind that, after all, for them their own methods of prayer *could* hold no effort, just because they were their own methods. They had discovered them for themselves, or God had discovered them to them; they were God-driven, not invented.

Poulain, for instance, says again that St. Teresa far excels all writers who preceded her on the subject of contemplation. In their descriptions, those prior to her confined themselves to generalities (excepting Angela de Foligno, Ruysbroeck and Marina d'Escobar, when describing their ecstasies). But St. Teresa was the first to give a clear, accurate and detailed classification. "After St. Teresa, the first place for careful observation of these matters belongs to St. John of the Cross. But his classifications are confused." As far as they them-selves were concerned, it was a case of:

> We were the first that ever burst
> Into that silent sea. . . .
>
> Alone, alone,—all, all alone:
> Alone on a wide, wide sea.

For a discoverer, when, that is, he sails across uncharted seas, there can in a sense be no strain of discovery. Interest, joy, thrill, a mounting *tempo* of hope and exultation, a rapture of adventure and enthusiasm, followed no doubt by moments of doubt and despondency : but that is not strain. He is tossed on the waves; now high, now low; but he is not directing them. The strain only arises from trying to follow

other people's charts, and that is what a good many of us do
when it comes to the matter of prayer. We keep on attempt-
ing to fit ourselves in, instead of letting ourselves out.

These particular saints were not the first to practise such
a form of prayer we may be fairly sure, but they were the
first to formulate it, each a little differently, and they did so
without effort because there was no effort of theirs behind
the prayer which they formulated. It just *was* their prayer:
the way along which God led them, and not the way along
which they led God.

So, in all the books written upon both meditation and
contemplation, we may be sure that we shall find something
which fits our own type, if we want to find it (and as a beginning it may be a good thing), just as one can find one's own
type of face or character, no doubt, if one is sufficiently interested.   There is the fair, calm style; the *petite*, vivacious
style; there are the recognized types of beauty and grace.
Into some sort of category of feature and temperament we are
bound to fall—but it is at this very point that the real differences begin. No two characters, and no two faces, are absolutely alike, but always have somewhere about them that
saving individuality which marks them as the work of God.

And so it is with our soul, and therefore with our prayer,
which is only the expression of the individual soul. When
one comes to think of it, it is as futile to set out to pray
in somebody else's style as it would be to attempt to talk
in the style of someone else, or to write bad poetry to the
moon because one admired the sonnets of some great poet.
All these things, if they are genuine, are completely individual,
and, in their own small way, unique. The fact that we may
come to a strange kind of void in our dealings with God, or
rather His dealings with us, does not mean that we have come
to the end of our prayer, but only probably that we have
come to the beginning of it.

What then, I ask myself, is it that so often prevents our
getting any further? The Sister who is going to ring the bell
for the hour of prayer gets up to leave the choir. In a few

minutes I hope that I may indeed be praying, instead of only thinking about it. Well then . . . ?

May it not perhaps be due to the obstacles which we are, sometimes quite unconsciously, interposing between ourselves and God? Unconsciously, not so much because we are not aware that these obstacles exist, but because it has not occurred to us to regard them as obstacles to union with God. All ways of prayer, and states of prayer, and diagnoses of prayer, will quite possibly melt, to our great spiritual comfort, before a simple attempt to get closer to God.

But then, how discover and remove the obstacles? It is really fairly straightforward work if we are absolutely honest with ourselves as to the attempt.

Is there anything which we have, and enjoy, either spiritually, mentally, or in actual material fact, which we would not give up to Him if He asked us for it? And by that one understands quite simply if it were taken from us either by the direct act of God or through the action of anyone else? Well, then. . . . Is there anything which we have not as yet got, which we feel that we absolutely must have; that our happiness depends upon it; that it is legitimate to bend all our efforts towards attaining it? Well, then . . . Is there anything false in our life anywhere; anything which does not ring quite true : which we only think of and acknowledge when we imagine ourselves to be alone? (Alone, I say to myself with emphasis, and not alone with God, for we should be ashamed of it before Him.) Well, then . . .

Let us set ourselves patiently to get rid of all those little dark spots in our souls and minds and spiritual lives, and then come back to our Lord, months or perhaps years on, and ask Him now to come and fill the place which we have tried to empty for Him. When we can look ourselves, and our neighbours, honestly in the face, knowing that there are no dusty corners which must not be disturbed concealed behind the glance of our eyes; no spider-web attachments binding our hearts to creatures and to earth; no hidden cavities of the mind into which we have thrust all those refusals and aversions which we dare not openly acknowledge: then we know that, although to God's all-seeing vision our heart is still not empty at all, but full of ourselves and every other misery, yet it is as empty as we, by His grace, have known how to make it, and we may humbly ask Him to finish the work for us.

Until He does, there is our void, our blank, the darkness of which the great spiritual writers speak. Until He does, we shall be sometimes overwhelmed with the inertia which weighs down the soul. If we have given up everything which we have, and which we knew how to give, how indeed could we be other than blinded and momentarily forlorn in the darkness of frustrated desire and the inertia of total loss?

7.40 p.m.

COMPLIN

A s we come down the stairs to the choir after recreation it is pleasant to know that the active day of work is over and that the best part of all, the silence and the uninterrupted prayer of night, is beginning. There was an old Sister in my Novitiate days who used to say that Complin, which she invariably recited by heart, was to her soul as the freshness of flowers in the spring. It is indeed the quietest of all the "Hours".

Originally it was introduced by St. Basil about the middle of the fourth century (for mention is made of it by Eusebius, St. Ambrose and Cassian) if not in its present more elaborate form, at all events in the form of prayers recited before retiring for that first sleep of the night which preceded the recitation of the night-office proper, that is Vigils (now

Matins and Lauds). It has always remained to me just that which our old Sister called it—a moment of delight, filled somehow with the freshness of violets and primroses and tall grass, and little running streams and the good-night song of birds.

The long and complete silence which follows it, silence, as far as creatures are concerned, until after the office of Prime of the next day, is the enclosed nun's time with God. All her day is filled with God too, of course, but it is filled with many other things as well; all seen, and undertaken, and completed in God, but nevertheless practical things which have to be seen and undertaken and completed.

Then comes Complin to set her soul free from earth; free in a sense from her community, for at least no one can talk to her until the morning (though in an emergency, and by sign, they may request some service); free for the God whom she came into the cloister to find in a sense in which she could not find Him out in the world.

" *Angeli tui sancti habitent in ea, qui nos in pace custodiant; et benedictio tua sit super nos semper.*"   And so the night begins.

8.10 p.m.

SUNSET AND DAWN

Up in our cell it is cool and quiet, and this is one of the happiest hours in the twenty-four. But when I am living them, I think each is the happiest. It is a free hour, like its sister the midday Silence, a time in which to work, to read, to pray, to walk in the garden on a summer evening: alone, silent, content. The sun is not yet really saying good night, but the shadows begin to fall across the green lawn under the window, while the trees stand motionless beneath the deepening blue of the sky. Later on it will turn to the real cloudless sapphire of night, and when I come up after Lauds, I know that the window will frame for me one of Whistler's Nocturnes in blue and silver.

Sitting on the window-seat in the clear stillness, one's thoughts turn instinctively to that other garden at Nazareth, the garden that Our Lady loved, and out upon which she must have looked upon many a summer evening. In thinking of Our Lady one cannot but think of her wonderful vocation and of the tiny reflected miniature of it which is ours. For if every priest is an *alter-Christi*, then surely every nun is, on the same human level, an *altera-Maria*?

So we come to the marvel of her earthly life and that part which she had to play, that is the perfect complementary rôle to her Divine Son. Was ever such a vocation before, could ever such a vocation be again? In the clear light of the centuries which have elasped since the enaction of that half-divine, half-human epic upon earth—Our Lady a woman yet the Mother of God—one realizes the marvel of her own quiet surrender to the divine; of the conquest of all that was most human in herself: a mother's love. In that wonderful duet which she was called upon to play, how she muted her strings until they sounded no more than a whisper behind the crash-splendour of His chords; how, her amazing yet simple and humble duty fulfilled, she faded into a background which yet shielded, guarded, and for many years was the home of the Master-Musician of the world. For our Lord's coming made music sound again on a silent earth, it woke to life and set vibrating once more all the broken strings of Man's nature—lost, forlorn, unredeemed.

Our Lady's part was a complementary part, but when it comes to ourselves and our imitation of her, we can hardly claim anything as wonderful as that. Perhaps, in our own case, it would be truer to say that we have a God-given vocation to play second fiddle. It *is* a vocation, and a delightful vocation, but all the same we shall do well to remember that a call to play second fiddle is not a call to go upon the shelf. Not by any means. The vocation to the shelf is something quite different and is not to be encouraged.

As a matter of fact, this vocation really scarcely exists nowadays, because it is so seldom offered to any but those who quite firmly decline to accept it; hence as a vocation it tends to become obsolete. As things are now, there is no fixed age whatsoever for retiring to the shelf, so that it is essentially—if a vocation at all—a very late vocation. Those who might be in a position to think that they now had a right to it are, in nine cases out of ten, mistaken, and the tenth case has no such ideas in its head at all and it is we who are making the mistake.

For their consolation let those who have a temptation to think longingly of the shelf remember that it is, after all, but a cobwebby sort of place, and that if only they will make one resolute effort and win their own individual battle against the inclination, they quite possibly may have another spell of real, useful work lying before them. The shelf is surely something which no one seriously considers nowadays, let us hope, except in moments of deep discouragement, and they should leave it for the jam, and sugar, and other pleasant things for which shelves are intended.

If they need any further persuasion, let them consider the difference between the added years which most probably lie before them, when spent in some useful fashion or spent upon the dusty shelf of their desire. The tangible gain in hours of work, of enjoyment, of kindness to others and happiness for themselves, may run into thousands, but the intangible gain will run into something which no one can assess at all. The difference between the person they will become during those final years of conquest and the person they would have been had they retired upstairs, is something which only God can value at its true estimate. But those who watch them can perhaps dimly sense it.

Shelves, however, are dull things to think about on a

summer evening and so I dismiss the thought with one final reflection : if anyone has been *put* on the shelf by force of circumstances over which they have no control, let them (which is usually the one thing on earth which they will not do) stay there gracefully. But if they merely desire, of their own weary inclination, to *climb* upon the shelf, and someone catches them by the leg and pulls them down again—let them *come* down again immediately, and as gracefully as may be, and make no more ado about it.

The vocation to second fiddle is a very different matter. It is a real vocation and one has it from birth. For a nun it is a vocation within a vocation and not every nun has it in itself, the real authentic aptitude, although the rôle of every nun is in a sense complementary. She is always filling up those things which are wanting, no matter whether she does it in a school, in a hospital, on the missionary field, in the slums, or behind iron bars in an enclosed convent.

The person with a real vocation to play second fiddle has to make no effort; one might almost unkindly say that there is no humility involved, for it is what she was created to do. A second fiddle who does not want to be a first violin, that is the rarity, and that is the authentic call for those who have it. The fact of not wanting anything else is the sign of the vocation, for of course one never does want anything else when one is doing what one was born to do. In one way every nun has to play second fiddle because of the marvel of the example of her prototype; but those with the true call play it because they love to play it—to fit in, to adapt, to accompany. It is a great art : not so showy, but just as real, as the art of the first violin.

To many another there is real virtue in self-effacement, in attempts at humility, in attempts at remaining in the background instead of taking the lead. That is very genuine virtue, and for those with a leader's temperament and disposition there could perhaps be no greater effort at holiness than the effort not to tell everyone else what to do and how to do it.

But these others have a different mission in life: a real mission. It is to back up, to support, to understand, to encourage; to be always at hand when wanted for any odd, insignificant job; to keep the more brilliant people going while seeming to do nothing at all.

Henry Thoreau explains in one of his books why he retired as a recluse to Walden. "I went to the woods because I wished to live deliberately, to front only the essential facts of life, and see if I could not learn what it had to teach, and not, when I came to die, discover that I had not lived. . . . Nor did I wish to practise resignation unless it was quite necessary."[1]

He pursued solitude as the enclosed nun pursues it: he went to the woods to play second fiddle to life itself, in order to discover the secrets of life. And hence his objection to mere resignation in face of them. Those who wish to learn —deep, deep learning—must always play second fiddle to the chosen teacher. So many of us, faced with this inscrutable mystery of earth, give it up and betake ourselves to that resigned attitude which is the death of all initiative, all endeavour, in a way to all the beauty of effort and creation. But Thoreau would first *front* the essential facts of life and set his will to learn their secret, before he gave up the hopeless task, sank his head upon his breast and became, as too many of us allow ourselves to become, merely their plaything.

A second fiddle goes deliberately into the shadow of the background in order to watch, to wait, to learn, to listen, as Thoreau watched and learnt from the wild life of Nature: but we—nuns—choose our solitude for the reason that we wish to learn the secrets of God, as Our Lady lived her retired life, silently watching her Son, and pondering many things in her heart. It was a willed retirement, a willed silence, not the silence and retirement of a coward in face of an agonizing and incomprehensible mystery.

And what happened in the case of Our Lady, and what happens often, in a minor degree, in the case of those who

[1] *Walden*, Henry Thoreau, p. 80.

follow her? The second fiddle becomes, all unbeknown to itself, the main support of the whole. I reached up to the little shelf where each of us may keep a few books for spiritual reading, and pulled down the volume of Henri de Lubac's *Meditation sur l'Eglise* (p. 293).

" If it is true that the Church is founded upon faith in its Saviour, then during the Passion, Mary, by the strength of her faith, supported and carried the whole edifice of the Church, like the strong timber-work upon which the entire structure rests. When she stood upright at the foot of the Cross, it was the Church which, in her Person, stood upright; on the night of Good Friday, while the faith of everyone else had, to say the least of it, grown dim, she embodied, in her indomitable faith, the faith of the Church of Christ itself. In the long Saturday vigil, while Christ slept in the tomb, the life of the Mystical Body withdrew as it were from sight and found refuge in her heart."

And so often that is the way with those whom we are perhaps inclined to push into the background as mere auxiliaries to the real business of life. We think of ourselves and of others in terms of broad achievement, and we forget all the thousand details which go to the making of it. Where should we ourselves perhaps be without that tiresome little point arranged for us, without that word of quiet encouragement just at the right moment, without that piece of practical advice which we had overlooked in our hurry, so unobtrusively given that we took it and acted upon it almost without noticing that it was not our own?

A happy vocation : a vocation which runs no risk of envy, either for itself or others, carries but little risk of pride in its train, and has a serene and deeply appreciative outlook upon all life.

I shut the book and prepare to go down to Matins at which, thank God, I am neither Hebdomadary nor Cantor, nor, so far as I know, have even a Lesson to read. The sound of the bell comes across the cool, green grass, comes reminding me of the origin of the office of Matins—or Lauds as it was originally called before the offices of Vigils and Matins were combined.

To me it is always something of a Chinese puzzle. Lauds was first called Matins and Matins was called Vigils; then Matins became Lauds, and Vigils Matins, and Vigils itself faded out altogether, but please do not ask me why. St. Benedict, however, as far as I can make out, stuck staunchly to his own way of calling things. So *he* always refers to Vigils as the night-office, whilst that of daybreak he calls Matins—Lauds being the last three psalms of that office. But if any Benedictine says that I am wrong then I should not hesitate to agree with him, because, to tell the truth, I have always had doubts myself. But at all events I am now going to choir to say all of them, one after the other, whatever they are called. " *That's* the way to do it—*that's* the way to do it," cries the blackbird from the top bough of the golden aspen. " Can't you take me too—can't you take me too? " I would take all the world with me if I could, and in my heart I do.

11 p.m.

AND SO—GOOD MORNING

A s I open wide the window of our cell, the white purity of the moon is reflected on to the whiteness of the walls, until the whole room is, as it were, drowned in white light which fills it with beauty. Somehow this—just this—is the beauty of earth as it has always seemed to me : as it does seem to some of us : changed and transformed by a mysterious radiance into something perennially marvellous.

That radiance transforms life for those of us who live by it, as this ordinary convent-garden is transformed by the silver shining of the moon upon it, the slight night-mist which rises and lends distance to its shrubs and winding paths, to the long, black shadows of the trees.

This is not the garden as we know the garden by daylight, and neither is our ideal life the actual life which we live out hour by hour. But this is the soul of the garden, and our ideal is the soul of life, perceived by our own souls, loved, enthroned for ever—and then marred for us, day after day, by actual events. Let us be patient. That does not matter: it does not matter at all. All that would matter would be if we allowed ourselves to be cast down by the fact, as we might foolishly be cast down to-morrow morning on perceiving that that little path to the left does not really lead over the edge of a hill, far up on to the Downs, nor that little streak of liquid silver really turn into a brook running towards the sea.

For our ideal is unattainable and must be—should be. We do, in truth, live by it, because our spirit lives by it, but our faulty human faculties lag behind. It is a dream, but a dream of Heaven without which our souls would faint away and die on this cold earth.

Even as I stand looking out of the window I realize how foolish this would sound to those who have never believed in a misty, moonlit garden—believed in it as real—never caught and held the truth behind the illusion.

There is no danger of confusion between the elusive yet satisfying reality of an ideal and that foolish, egocentric day-dreaming which is to be avoided like the pest. The latter leads us continually back to self; the former leads us continually away from it. It is a striving for something beyond earth, something infinitely above us, something momentarily out of the reach of purely human capacity, but already within the capacity of the soul. The realization of it is something not for to-day but for to-morrow—yet something without which we could not live to-day as to-day should be lived.

And the price of the ideal? What is the price? The price, I think, is suffering—but the kind of suffering which is never, for one moment, to be confused with unhappiness. It is a debt due to God—a debt due to life. It does not matter where the suffering comes from, through whom, or how. If it were not this particular suffering, it would be other suffering, so what matter? There is a debt, a debt to God, to life, to the eternal, which can only be paid in suffering, as one might owe a debt which could only be paid in dollars, sterling being of no use.

This price, the price of the ideal, is not personal. It is a general price for a general debt: the debt of all mankind to God, who gave to each a soul and, by the agony of the Cross, redeemed that soul when it strayed from Him.

Who would barter such suffering, such a debt, for all the fleeting happiness which earth might have to offer? For us, the passing pleasures of life are themselves but an illusion. When we had enjoyed them to the full, when we had sold our birthright for our brother's mess of potage, what should we do then? When we found ourselves old at last; when life had lost its zest; when we began to feel the decay of all for which we had bartered our youth's ideal—what should we feel like then? I wonder.

Fools, cheated even here on earth of the fulfilment of our earthly desires: not cheated, as we had meant to cheat *ourselves*, of the passing pleasures of life for love of God and for the sake of life eternal; but cheated in truth and for ever, of all that we might have done, might have been. A moonlit illusion? Beauty is never an illusion; endeavour is never an illusion; the cleansing of the spirit by courageous suffering is never an illusion; and Christ, and the ideal which He came to bring to earth, His Passion, His Death, His Redemption of us, are never illusions.

In the far distance I hear the sound of my friends the aeroplanes. The sound is so familiar that it has grown right into the very woof of my nights. They taxi down the runway, and for each in turn there comes that crucial moment, the moment when my heart too always seems to take a little upward leap with them as they become airborne.

Sometime, I say to myself, that moment will come for all of us: the moment when our hearts take flight to God, never to return. But that, fellow-pilgrims, is not just yet. There is still life to be lived. And here, waiting for us on tiptoe as the clock strikes twelve, waiting with all its joys and its battles and the brimming fulness of the love of God is—To-morrow.